REINVENTING
YOU

Praise for

REINVENTING YOU
THE 10 BEST WAYS *to* LAUNCH YOUR DREAM CAREER

I have seen reinvention in many forms, including my own personal life. Lisa Lockwood is second to none in understanding life reinvention. She lives it, can relate to it, and helps thousands of people experience their own reinventions every year. Reinventing YOU is the go to guide to making major changes in your life starting day one. You are in for something far more than you could imagine.

—**Chris Foltz**, Internationally Renowned Social Impact Strategist and founder of Christopher Foltz Collaborative, L3C

Who at one point in their life has not wanted to switch things up? Who hasn't wanted to embark on a journey of self improvement? Who hasn't wanted to experience life on a higher or completely different level? I believe we all have and if you haven't, sooner or later you will! I know of no greater authority on self-reinvention than Lisa Lockwood. Her personal transformations have been absolutely remarkable. If you're stuck and want to break free, or if you are already well on a journey of reinvention in your own life, Lockwood's book is the inspirational catalyst for the most amazing life you can have. More than anything, the reader will learn that they can do and accomplish anything they need, crave or desire--at any stage of life!

—**Paul Edgewater**, International Best-Selling Author, Co-Founder/CMO BusyBeePromotions.com and America's Promotions Powerhouse™

Lisa Lockwood will help you find the BLESS in any MESS so you can move forward and enjoy the rest of your life in joy and in celebration of your gifts and talents. Lisa is a 'PROFIT PROPHET' and can help you speed up your results and boost your bottom line.

—**Barry Spilchuk,** Author — *THE cancer DANCE*
Coauthor — *A Cup of Chicken Soup for the Soul*
www.THEcancerDANCE.com

Lisa Lockwood is that rare pearl we each hope to find... After working with her for over a decade, she never ceases to amaze me. Not only has she served as a guiding light and inspiration to me personally but she has consistently given of herself to help thousands reinvent themselves in a turbulent and changing world. She has a gift and I'm so fortunate to have been one of so many who have been blessed by her influence and her passion. Lisa's new book is a must read if you're looking for a breakthrough!

—**Wilson Ramcharan**, Marketing & Events Coordinator WJR Enterprises

REINVENTING
YOU

THE 10 BEST WAYS
to LAUNCH YOUR
DREAM CAREER

LISA LOCKWOOD

THE REINVENTION EXPERT

NEW YORK

REINVENTING YOU
THE 10 BEST WAYS *to* LAUNCH YOUR DREAM CAREER

© 2014 **LISA LOCKWOOD**.

Published in New York, New York, by Morgan James Publishing. Morgan James and The Entrepreneurial Publisher are trademarks of Morgan James, LLC.
www.MorganJamesPublishing.com

The Morgan James Speakers Group can bring authors to your live event. For more information or to book an event visit The Morgan James Speakers Group at www.TheMorganJamesSpeakersGroup.com.

BitLit
FOR ALL THE BOOKS YOU OWN

FREE eBook edition for your existing eReader with purchase

PRINT NAME ABOVE

For more information, instructions, restrictions, and to register your copy, go to **www.bitlit.ca/readers/register** or use your QR Reader to scan the barcode:

ISBN 978-1-61448-550-6 paperback
ISBN 978-1-61448-857-6 hard cover
ISBN 978-1-61448-551-3 eBook
ISBN 978-1-61448-552-0 audio
Library of Congress Control Number:
2013945472

Cover Design by:
Rachel Lopez
www.r2cdesign.com

Interior Design by:
Bonnie Bushman
bonnie@caboodlegraphics.com

In an effort to support local communities, raise awareness and funds, Morgan James Publishing donates a percentage of all book sales for the life of each book to Habitat for Humanity Peninsula and Greater Williamsburg.

Get involved today, visit
www.MorganJamesBuilds.com

Habitat
for Humanity®
Peninsula and
Greater Williamsburg
Building Partner

To God—the universal source energy I strive to emulate, for giving me the gift of this amazing human experience.

To my parents—Don and Darlene Lockwood. Thank you for teaching me so many valuable life lessons. I love you both very much!

To my sister—Michelle DiCola. You are my number-one, life-long fan, best friend, and the most selfless and generous person I have ever met. I love you!

To my editor—Michele Budka (a.k.a. Girl Friday). Thank you for not only being so skilled in your profession, but for being such a beautiful person, supporter, and cheerleader for the past six plus years!

Finally, to all of my coaching clients. Thank you for having the courage to trust me with your most personal and intimate life experiences. You have given me more gifts than you can possibly imagine.

CONTENTS

We are capable of achieving things far greater than we think. It is only our perceived limitations that prevent us from stepping into our next reinvention.

—Lisa Lockwood

PREFACE

Reinventing YOU is an action plan for taking your life in a new direction. It is about discovering how you can shape your future by acknowledging your accomplishments, attaching new meanings to not-so-great life events, and embracing high standards for yourself in order to fulfill your life's mission. In short, *Reinventing YOU* will help you chart your true course in life!

People reinvent themselves for different reasons—to have a better life, be more respected, make more money, be happier, develop a stronger body, build better relationships, get to know God, or to have a more fulfilling life.

If your ears perk up when you hear about the lawyer who gave it all up to become a fashion designer, or the auditor who ditched her accounting firm to start her own pet clothing company, and wonder how they did it, this book is for you. You will discover what is typical and what is rare among people who attempt to reinvent themselves—the person who yearns for change but remains stuck and the person who leaves it all for something completely different.

We've all known people who have ditched their successful careers, and the stability of the lives they've created, to go in a new direction and become something or someone else. It is not easy nor is it safe, so why do people do it? What motivates them to make the leap to get back on track and pursue their unfulfilled dreams and potential? Sometimes, it's a reflection of how they have changed. What you want or need now in your life may be very different from what you wanted when you were just starting out. To be fulfilled, you will find a need to reinvent yourself many times throughout your life.

We have all already reinvented ourselves at some point in our lives. Sometimes, it is a more discretionary, calculated choice we make, like pursuing a dream. Other times, external factors force us to change. We become a caregiver for an aging parent, or find ourselves the victim of a crime, or dealing with a health crisis.

When circumstances are outside of our control, our reinvention is *a must*. When we're contemplating making a shift to pursue a goal or dream, we often categorize it as a "should". But shouldn't we also classify our goals and dreams as "musts"? The answer is absolutely, positively YES!

Think about how quickly we reinvent ourselves during a crisis. We barely have time to think, let alone choose. Imagine that you are going about your life, showing up at work, taking care of the kids and the house and then WHAM, catastrophe strikes. Your world is turned upside down, and you are forced to surrender to your new role. You prioritize your life based on an external event and all other matters are no longer important.

Choosing to be "at cause" for a reinvention does not rate very high for most people. We find we're better at clean up than we are at putting our energy and attention on creating what we truly want.

Take it from me—a welfare kid, waitress, beauty queen, abused woman, heavy equipment operator, Desert Storm veteran, police officer, undercover detective, SWAT team member, author, speaker, career coach, professor and step-mom—we are not what we do. We are the result of the *meanings* we attached to the compilation of our life experiences. Every door opened to us and closed behind us, represents an opportunity for reinvention.

How many times have you heard people who have had a difficult childhood, or experiences as an adult say, "It was because of those challenges that I became stronger."? Or "Those challenges shaped my life." Or "I would not change my past for anything."

There is value in every life experience if we permit ourselves to look for the gift we received from those events.

How you do that depends on the meanings you attach to each event. When I did not win the Miss Illinois Pageant, I changed my life course. Swimming pools and movie stars needed to wait. I was eighteen years old;

there was still plenty of time for that. If I had not joined the military, I may not have obtained the benefits of, "There is no I in team" or added personal accountability, perseverance, drive and persistence to my expanding identity.

It's easy to look for what is *not* working in our lives and even easier to find people to join our pity party. Misery loves company, right? I am the opposite. I have a need to bring people up and discovered a knack for finding ways to turn every unfortunate circumstance into something funny and positive. That is my method for shift. I want to help you discover the method that works best for you.

I've set up this book in a way I believe will give you the most value. In each chapter, I will share a story and a strategy on how I've coached clients and how I've used the strategy in my own life. Tools and exercises after each chapter will allow your learning to become deeply ingrained into your psyche. You will also be inspired by stories about political figures, celebrities, athletes, innovators and spiritual leaders who have used these tools and strategies to shape their own reinventions. Reading biographies of people you admire, who are getting the results you want, is a great way to get a jump-start on getting the results you are after.

It was imperative for me when I was a police detective to ask the right questions to get to the root of a situation as fast as possible. Now, as a coach, I utilize my experience as a detective to get to the root of what people are seeking in order to help them find fulfillment in their lives. So let's get started finding yours!

The two most important days of your life are the day you were born and the day you found out why.

—Mark Twain

• *Chapter One* •

WHAT IS REINVENTION?

#1 Mastering Your Emotions

C hange is life's only true constant. When we resist change, we take on the most powerful force in the universe. When we fight against it, we are self-defeating.

There are two main reasons why people change. These things force most of us to reinvent ourselves:

1. **Calculated choice**-Pursuing a goal deliberately and with foresight.
2. **Forced**-Out of necessity, due to external factors (ending a relationship, becoming the victim of a crime, financially strapped, failing health, company downsizing).

Depending on where we are emotionally, financially, or physically, a catalyst for reinvention is born.

Most people reinvent themselves when they are forced to out of necessity. I'd love for you to embrace reinvention on *purpose*. Allow your cause and your purpose to become the new *must* for the new and improved you!

In this book, I will delve into life reinvention strategies and career reinventions. Most people identify themselves based on what they do versus who they are. The two actually go hand-in-hand.

"We have found a direct correlation in career happiness to overall happiness in life," says Matt Miller, chief technology officer at CareerBliss. "Stress at work, for example, can often carry over to stress at home."

I was invited to be a guest on the Steve Harvey Show in Chicago to coach three people who had careers that made the top ten unhappiest jobs list of 2012. My role was to find out if they wanted to leave their careers and completely reinvent themselves, or figure out a way to make their current environment happier.

Here is the top ten list followed by a transcript of the Steve Harvey Show interview:

Unhappiest Jobs 2012:
1. Security Officer
2. Registered Nurse
3. Teacher
4. Sales Engineer
5. Product Manager
6. Program Manager
7. Marketing Manager
8. Director of Sales
9. Marketing Director
10. Maintenance Supervisor

Steve: Today we are going to talk about why some of these jobs are said to be the unhappiest. Welcoming unhappiest professionals—Erica, Justin, and Svetlana.

Steve: Erica you were a teacher which was number three on the list. What was tough about it in the classroom?

Erica: First, I love children. I also think teachers are underpaid for all of the molding of young minds they do. Much of the time I felt unhappy and feeling like I was babysitting.

Steve: You left teaching, and you are now a flight attendant, are you happy?

Erica: Some days, though now the job has grown up kids. I saw an ad in the paper and thought for the heck of it I'll give it a try. I found people still disrespected me and talked to me like I was crazy. Often I needed to bite my tongue.

Steve: Justin you wanted to be a cop, but got into a car accident, and now you are a security guard.

Justin: It's not as great as being a cop, getting called names like "rent-a-cop" or "bully". The general consensus on how we are viewed is we're there to ruin their good times at places like festivals, sporting events, or concerts.

Svetlana: I'm a nurse for a trauma/intensive care unit. It's a high stress job, and we're often treated like maids or waitresses. We're verbally abused on a daily basis. I've gotten bit, spit on, kicked.

Steve: Fix things to make it work. Today I have invited reinvention coach, Lisa Lockwood. Lisa you are a reinvention coach for life. Tell us exactly what you do.

Lisa: I help people who are unhappy in their careers, who are transitioning, not a hundred percent sure what they want to do, but they know what they don't want to do. I went from heavy equipment operator in Desert Storm, to an undercover police officer posed as a stripper. I know the stresses. I know what you're going through and I want to help you.

Steve: Do you think these three people can find happiness in their work?

Lisa: I absolutely do, and everybody watching today as well. I'm going to share some strategies that I think you're going to be happy about.

Steve: It's not economically realistic for people to quit their jobs right now because there aren't a lot of jobs out there. So if you're looking to make a career change, where do you start?

Lisa: That's a super question. What people need to acknowledge is that two thirds of American's are unhappy in their jobs. That's a huge number, and what I encourage people to do is not just leave their job on a whim, it's discovering what they need to do in the process so they get their feet wet. What I also do is offer coping strategies.

Steve: So how can people cope at work when they are unhappy?

Lisa: First thing is you need to develop a thick skin. There are going to be some things that are out of your control. What I used to do is show up happy at work with a completely optimistic disposition and it takes the wind away from people. The next thing is imagine you're financially free. Now, if you're at home thinking what am I going to do with my life, if you had all the money in the world, what would you be excited about every day, saying I get to do this? I don't want just to create mindset strategies. In your current position what can you do to make your job more fun and exciting? Be creative. I offer exercises and this one exercise is actually called a butt clinch. Two benefits, you're focusing on your butt, and you're squeezing it, what that does is allow you to breathe in. So what I recommend is you take breaths with it. Count in your mind. One one thousand, two one thousand, three one thousand. Can we do this together? When you're in front of people you get distracted, so you really gotta focus on that clinch and holding it helps your breathing, but guess what else? It also helps firm your glutes!

Steve: Ok, so give us another one.

Lisa: The next one is pressure points, acupressure. Take your hand, and you press right between your index finger and your thumb until you feel just a little bit of pain. This is a reliever for headaches, but it also stimulates your circulatory system and it takes away the edge.

The first two I gave you are for when you're in a scenario, and you can't escape in order to vent. So this one is when you're on your job. I recommend going into a parking lot, or a storage closet, go into the ladies room and lock the door. It's called a power move.

Basically, what I want you to do is, pretend you're a superhero. So in your mind you're a superhero, getting ready to combat something. I'm gonna show you mine to give you an example. What I do is I rev myself up (makes kick boxing motions) then I regroup and go back to work. That's it.

Steve: I want to see everyone's power moves, so pretend like you're in the bathroom (everyone fake fights). Our guests could really use some one-on-one guidance. Let's start with Erica, going from one unhappy job to the next.

Lisa: Erica, I really get that you love children, and that's kind of your core and what your calling is. I think you also like travel. So combining the two together would be your own business "Erica's Private Tutoring on the Road." Another thing I think would be amazing with your traveling as well would be teaching children English as a second language.

Lisa: So Justin, one of the things I think would be amazing that would give you a little bit of the police experience as well is a 911 dispatcher. If you did decide you want to stay in security, I would recommend doing something that's a little higher up in the line, maybe on a cruise ship.

Lisa: Svetlana, in order to get away from the patient after care and all the stress you have to deal with, I was thinking what would be really cool for you is to be an EMT/First Responder. You're not dealing with all the family members and things like that. And another thing I thought of is "Nurses Without Borders". You get to travel, and you also have that opportunity of working with people again, doing what your career is rather than going back to get education to do something else.

Steve: When it comes to your career you can dream big, but you can't do anything without a plan of action. You can't make a career change without first exploring all your options. So I've compiled a list of contacts and job opportunities for each of our guests today.

Overall, the Steve Harvey Show was a great example of how important it is to look at challenges from a different perspective and realize that you're not alone in your struggles.

Let's take a look at two successful western society icons, Madonna and Oprah. First, I want to highlight the Queen of Reinvention, Madonna. I want to show you one of the most high profile examples of how Madonna reinvented herself repeatedly at breakneck speed to remain current.

Whether you like Madonna or not, her successful music career is not her only highlight in life. Madonna's unparalleled ability to reinvent herself over the last three decades places her in a league of her own when it comes to reinvention.

Madonna

Madonna was only five years old when her mother died of breast cancer at the young age of thirty. This loss significantly affected her childhood.

Haunted by the memories of her dying mother's passive frailty, she vowed to make her mark on the world.

"The biggest reason I was able to express myself, and not be intimidated, was not having a mother," she says. "Mothers teach you manners, and I absolutely did not learn any of those."

She fought against rules imposed by her stepmother, Joan Gustafson, once the family's housekeeper. Forced to care for her younger siblings, she resented the task. "I saw myself as the quintessential Cinderella." She rebelled, creatively turning her clothing into revealing outfits, dancing at underground gay nightclubs, and rejecting her family's religious beliefs.

Madonna developed a drive for perfectionism too and was a high achiever. A straight-A student, cheerleader, and talented dancer, she graduated high school a semester early. Her discipline and hard work paid off when she earned a full scholarship to the University of Michigan's dance program.

During her undergraduate studies, she was awarded a rare chance to study with the Alvin Ailey American Dance Theater in New York. At the urging of her dance instructor, the determined young Madonna dropped out of college to move to New York and pursue her dreams.

In New York, Madonna worked odd jobs to pay the rent—nude art model; server at the Russian Tea Room; and dancer with the American Dance Center. Musician Dan Gilroy, her boyfriend at the time, introduced her to the director of a vaudeville review in Paris, and she moved to France to work as a showgirl, falling in love with the combination of singing, dancing, and acting. When she returned to the US, she joined Gilroy's band as the drummer, eventually becoming lead singer. Hungry for more, Madonna formed several bands of her own during this time—Madonna & The Sky, The Millionaires, and Emmy.

In 1981, Madonna went solo, hiring manager Camille Barbone of Gotham Records who taught her how to navigate the male-dominated music business and put together a studio band accentuating her hip musical style. Stephen Bray, a musician in Madonna's band, wrote her first hit, "Everybody" and Madonna used her tough business sense to get the track to producer Mark Kamins who helped her land a recording contract with Sire Records. "Everybody" was an instant hit, going all the way to number one on the dance charts.

Using this success to her advantage, Madonna convinced Sire Records to produce the album, *Madonna,* which included the hit singles "Borderline", "Lucky Star", and "Holiday." Girls all over the country imitated Madonna's distinct fashions—fishnet stockings, lace lingerie worn as clothing, fingerless gloves, and large crucifix necklaces. During an interview on Dick Clark's *American Bandstand,* she told Clark her main ambition was to rule the world. She was on her way.

Like a Virgin, her next album, hit number one on the Billboard Chart and went platinum in under a month. She starred in her first film, *Desperately Seeking Susan,* and performed the soundtrack's single, "Into the Groove," which became an overnight hit. Her next single "Crazy for You", from the film *Vision Quest,* went number one too and, while on her first concert tour, she watched seventeen songs make it into the top ten on the music charts.

In 1985, she married actor Sean Penn and co-starred in the film *Shanghai Surprise.* She starred in three more movies during the 80s—*Who's That Girl?, Bloodhounds of Broadway* and *Dick Tracy.* Music from *Dick Tracy* resulted in the hits "Vogue" and "Hanky Panky". Still driven to push even higher, she produced four more hit albums: *True Blue, Who's that Girl?, You Can Dance,* and *Like a Prayer.*

Madonna never stopped mixing her drive for success with her love of scandalous behavior. She performed her hit single "Like a Virgin" on the MTV music awards, writhing suggestively onstage in a wedding dress. Her marriage to Sean Penn—accused of domestic violence and assaulting a photographer, behavior that landed him a month's jail time and led to his very public divorce—raised eyebrows. Madonna's video for "Like a Prayer" was banned in several countries despite being part of a lucrative Pepsi endorsement.

Madonna became more popular than ever. By 1991, she achieved twenty-one top ten hits in the US, selling more than seventy million albums internationally. She helped found Maverick Records, under the Warner Music Group, in 1992.

She continued to push social boundaries with the film *Truth or Dare,* a revealing documentary about her Blonde Ambition concert tour. *Sex,* a soft-core pornographic coffee-table book featuring the star in a variety of nude and erotic pictures, sparked a worldwide controversy yet sold 150,000 copies the day it was released in the US. In three days, all 1.5

million copies of the first edition sold out worldwide, making it the most successful coffee table book ever released. Her album, *Erotica* unveiled at the same time, reached the double-platinum status.

Proving her versatility as a performer in film and music, she starred in the critically acclaimed film adaptation of Andrew Lloyd Webber's musical *Evita*, winning a Golden Globe award for best performance by an actress in a motion picture. The song, "You Must Love Me," earned her an Academy Award for best original song. She gave birth that same year to her daughter, Lourdes Maria (Lola) Ciccone Leon, whose father was Madonna's lover and personal trainer, Carlos Leon.

Reinventing herself yet again, into a more mature, family-friendly Madonna, she married British director Guy Ritchie in 2000 and gave birth to their son, Rocco John Ritchie, the same year. She went on to star in the London stage play *Up for Grabs*, and wrote her first children's book, *The English Roses*, for her daughter.

Inducted into the UK Music Hall of Fame after she became the artist with the most gold-certified hit singles in the US, she beat the Beatles long-standing record.

Just before her 50th birthday, Madonna adopted a boy from Malawi, and added to her family again in 2009 when she was granted custody of Mercy James.

Reaching the height of her success in 2008, she was named the world's wealthiest female musician by *Forbes* magazine, with estimated earnings of more than $72 million, earning much of her income from her H&M clothing line; a televised concert deal with NBC, and her *Confessions* tour—the highest-grossing concert tour by a female artist in history. She continued to sing, act, and manage a variety of business interests while dividing her time between the UK and the US. She wrote and produced *I Am Because We Are* a documentary about the lives of Malawi's AIDS orphans, and the art house film *Filth and Wisdom*. Her *Sticky and Sweet* tour became her first joint venture with Live Nation.

Soon after, *Celebration* became Madonna's eleventh number one album in the UK, and she tied Elvis Presley as the solo act with the most number one albums in the UK.

In 2011, Madonna released her film *W.E.* about American divorcee Wallis Simpson and Britain's King Edward VIII, who gave up his crown to marry Simpson. Working behind the camera for the first time, Madonna directed and co-wrote the romantic drama. Despite receiving mixed reviews, she won a Golden Globe award for the original song she wrote for the film.

At fifty-four, Madonna performed during the half-time show for Super Bowl XLVI in 2012, just before the release of her album *MDNA* and doesn't seem anywhere close to stopping her reinventions.

What pattern do you notice reading Madonna's bio? You probably noted that she has an exorbitant amount of passion and drive. When people are passionate about doing what they love, success inevitably follows.

People have patterns. If you take a long hard look at your life, you will see that, through those patterns, you are able to see why you get the results you do in our life. And you can begin to make changes. You can reinvent.

Have you had more than ten jobs in your life? More than fifteen? How about upwards of twenty?

If you are in your forties, having held at least fifteen jobs is considered the norm. Out of those jobs, how many did you want to do instead of feeling you had to do them out of necessity?

Take a trip down memory lane. Use the spaces provided to write down every job you remember. In the second column, write down if you did it because you wanted to do it or because you felt you had to do it.

Job Title	Wanted to or had to?

We've all had to reinvent ourselves in the employment arena in order to fulfill a need. Look at your needs, and think about the times in your life that you had them. Did they motivate you to achieve something? To earn a living? To pursue your dream career? To save up to buy something?

We change, shift, and transform because we want to or because we feel that we *need* to. Both ways serve us, especially when we have an end or goal in mind. But wouldn't it be nice to have the choice of what you would like to do next? Wouldn't it be nice to do what you want to do instead of what you have to do?

Look back at your answers above and notice how many times you have reinvented yourself because you "had to" compared to the number of times you "wanted to" because you intentionally set out for reinvention. Evaluate who has been designing your life, you or the influence from your immediate environment?

Whatever it is that you want out of life, it cannot happen without reinventing yourself. If you worry that you cannot do it, take a look at your answers above again and see that you have already reinvented yourself multiple times in your life whether you realize it or not. Reinvention happens with or without your approval.

Considering what you learned from Madonna's path, look at Oprah Winfrey's journey through more educated eyes.

> *The whole point of being alive is to evolve into the complete person you were intended to be.*
> —**Oprah Winfrey**

Oprah Winfrey

After a troubled childhood in a small farming community, where she was sexually abused by several relatives, Oprah Gail Winfrey moved to Nashville to live with her father and attend Tennessee State University. It was here she began working in radio and television broadcasting.

In 1976, Oprah was invited to Baltimore to host the TV talk show *People Are Talking.* She turned the show into a hit, gaining the attention of Chicago's ABC affiliate who recruited her to host their morning show *A.M. Chicago* airing against the wildly popular Phil Donahue. Within months, Winfrey's warm-hearted, down-to-earth personality earned her 100,000 more viewers than Donahue. Her show went from last to first place in the ratings, and her success led to a coveted role in Steven Spielberg's film *The Color Purple*. Oprah capped off this achievement by earning a Motion Picture Academy award nomination for best supporting actress.

Soon after, she went nationwide launching *The Oprah Winfrey Show* on 120 channels. With its audience of ten million people, the show grossed $125 million by the end of the year, netting Oprah a $30 million payday. She gained ownership of the program, under the control of her new production company, Harpo (Oprah spelled backwards) Productions and began making lucrative syndication deals.

With talk shows becoming increasingly exploitative, Oprah kept hers free of tabloid-like topics. Though her ratings initially dropped, she earned the respect of her audience and an upsurge in popularity, starring in the Harpo Productions produced highly rated, TV miniseries *The Women of Brewster Place* and signing a multi-picture contract with Disney.

Oprah became almost as famous for her struggles with weight as for her talk show and acting careers, losing an estimated ninety pounds and capping off the achievement by completing the Marine Corps Marathon in Washington, DC. Riding the wake of her success, her personal chef Rosie Daley, and fitness and diet trainer Bob Greene, published best-selling books.

Oprah became a media mogul when she launched "Oprah's Book Club" on her talk show, propelling many new authors to bestseller status. She is often credited with giving reading a newfound, popular prominence in US culture. Her highly successful magazine *O: The Oprah Magazine* debuted in 2000.

Oxygen Media, the company she co-founded, produces cable and Internet programming for women. She is one of the most powerful and wealthy people in the business. In 2002, she inked a deal putting her show on prime time TV and, only two years later, she signed a contract to host *The Oprah Winfrey Show* through the 2010-11 season announcing that she would end her program when the contract expired.

According to *Forbes*, Oprah was the richest African American of the twentieth century. *Life* called her the most influential woman of her generation. *Business Week* named her the greatest black philanthropist in American history after her Angel Network raised more than $51,000,000 for charitable programs.

Oprah used her fame to become a respected activist for children's rights, convincing President Clinton to sign a bill into law creating a shared national database of convicted child abusers. In 2002, Oprah was honored as the first recipient of The Academy of Television Arts and Sciences Bob Hope Humanitarian Award.

Her campaign appearances for Barack Obama during the 2007 Democratic Presidential race attracted the largest crowds of the contest; 29,000 supporters attended a rally at the University of South Carolina football stadium alone. "Dr. Martin Luther King dreamed the dream. But we don't have to just dream the dream anymore," Oprah told the crowd. "We get to vote that dream into reality by supporting a man who knows not just who we are, but who we can be." The power of her endorsement was clear when Obama won the race to become the first African American President in US history.

When *The Oprah Winfrey Show* ended in 2011, Oprah formed the TV network *The Oprah Winfrey Network (OWN)*.

Engaged to Stedman Graham, public relations executive, since 1992 Oprah divides her time between California, Indiana, and Colorado.

What do Oprah and Madonna have in common? They applied the ten secrets you will learn in this book. This is the common thread among the modern-day leaders and visionaries I've chosen to share with you.

> *We are shaped by our thoughts. We become what we think.*
>
> **—Buddha**

How to Reinvent

Successful reinvention begins with mastering your emotions. Your emotional state will determine your success or failure. When I refer to your emotions, I'm also referring to your state of mind. Being happy or joyful does not mean that everything is perfect. It means you have decided to look beyond the imperfections in your environment and shift your focus to all that is good or what could be good.

Our emotions, feelings and beliefs about our life experiences are what makes or breaks our state of mind. Before I delve into callings, or careers or relationships, it is essential for you to know how important it is to master your emotions because your overall well-being affects every aspect of your life.

I used many of the "10 best ways" I'm sharing with you in this book to assist me through the compounded pain emanating from the tragic death of my beloved dog, a two-year-old Maltese named Pinky, and the decision to end my second marriage. Through all of the challenging experiences in my life, these two events top the list for the most emotionally painful.

Pinky

In May of 2011, I was abruptly awakened by my husband screaming, "Nooooo!"

I jumped from bed, and ran to find him in the living room. He knelt over our beloved Pinky, on her side, immobile, but breathing. While he was loading his car, he left the house door open. He heard her yelp from the street when she was hit by a car. He expressed his grief, and I shifted into a robotic mode I can only attribute to my military and police training. I rapidly dressed, scooped up my wounded dog in a blanket and then jumped into my car, starting the engine.

My husband followed me, torn between coming along to the veterinarian and continuing to his business event in another city. I didn't give him an option and insisted he accompany us. He jumped in the car and drove, weeping, "Oh my God, I'm so sorry," for the entire drive to the clinic.

All the while, I cradled Pinky in my arms and said over and over, "It's okay, baby girl. I love you." I offered prayers to God.

At the clinic, we turned Pinky over to the medical team and waited in the lobby. Still in a state of shock, I sat in the lobby and half listened to my husband explain that he couldn't miss his business event. He made sure I had money for a cab and subsequently left for his business meeting. I was too distraught this time to fight for him to stay with me.

Alone and grief stricken my subconscious mind caught up with my conscious, I held my stomach and cried my heart out. The staff asked if they could phone anyone to be with me. My family was in Chicago, so I contacted my mother-in-law who met me at the clinic.

A short while later, we were brought into the examination room and told Pinky was no longer with us. I could not comprehend that was even possible. During this time, my husband phoned the clinic and learned that Pinky had passed away, and returned to be with me. They gave us an opportunity to say our final goodbyes. Her body was still warm and she looked pristine in spite of being hit by a car. She had no sign of outward injury.

Everyone deals with grief differently. My husband fell to his knees, retreating into his own world, in no position to offer me solace. I wept and stroked her lifeless body from head to tail, telling her how much she meant to me and how much I loved her, thanking her for coming into my life.

Back at home, I had a brief conversation with my mother and sister in Chicago. I asked my mother-in-law to go around the house and gather all of Pinky's toys, beds, and food bowls, so they weren't in my sight. I crawled into bed, hoping to fall asleep and wake-up again to find it had all been just a nightmare.

The days and weeks following were a blur to me. My sister, Michelle flew to town to support my family and me. I oscillated between depressive bouts consisting of breakdowns, little sleep and no appetite, to half-heartedly rallying myself to watch funny movies, getting massages and spa treatments. I knew that I was not taking care of myself the best way I knew how, and I didn't care. My emotional state sank so low that on many evenings, before falling asleep, I wished I didn't have to wake up and feel the pain of another day without Pinky.

Friends and family members did everything they could to support me, even recommending a replacement. A replacement! The thought of replacing Pinky was unfathomable. After going along for a visit to the pet store and a shelter, I became even more grief stricken. I grieved her just as hard as I loved her.

About a week later, I experienced a shift. I sought out spiritual guidance and decided to focus on all of the things I loved and felt grateful for about Pinky. In a synchronistic way, I bumped into a woman I revered for her peaceful, loving spirit. She knew how much I loved Pinky and was not aware that I had lost her. When I gave her the news, I became choked up.

She embraced me, and said, "This is good Lisa."

I could not imagine what she thought was good. Was it good that I was letting my emotion flow or was it good that I lost Pinky? After gathering myself, I asked, "What do you mean?"

She explained, "Pinky was brought to you to show you love and give you joy. She served her purpose. She is an angel and was never meant to stay with you forever. Angels like Pinky have their own journeys. She is still part of this world and will forever live in your heart."

My blood rushed through me in a whoosh, leaving my body tingling. In that moment, I did feel Pinky in my heart. I began to cry tears of gratitude.

I chose to believe her words because they resonated with me in an inexplicable way—the way the sense of knowing can take over you when you just know that something is right.

Because of that encounter, I knew there must be another angel Pinky just waiting to be part of our lives. We began to search for her. Within a short period, we welcomed ten week old, baby Pinky II into our lives.

I never experienced that kind of grief in my life. I didn't choose that experience to reinvent my life. It chose me. Remember, we reinvent ourselves most often because we choose to or because we're forced to. Can you see that this reinvention experience was out of necessity? It was an opportunity to expand myself in a way I've never experienced. Once I was able to attach a new meaning to the event, I was able to shift my emotional state into one that would serve me better.

> *When you're going through hell, keep going.*
> **—Sir Winston Churchill**

The Divorce

In mid-June, during my Pinky grieving period, I told my husband, the man I had often referred to as my soul mate, "I want a divorce."

Uttering those words came as a shock to both of us. We had devoted a large part of our lives to personal growth. We studied and applied the things we felt were important in maintaining and enhancing a healthy relationship. We even hosted several relationship seminars, sharing tips and strategies we felt served our relationship.

We agreed to seek relationship counseling. After several co-sessions and individual sessions, it was clear to me that our values were no longer in alignment and divorce proceedings were initiated. Neither of us wanted to vacate our home; thus, our stress filled, three-month long co-habitation began.

Out of respect for the privacy of my former husband, and my three amazing stepchildren who I had the honor of sharing eight and a half years of my life, I will refrain from disclosing the details of those stressors. What is important to reveal are some of the methods and tools I used to cope.

My emotional spirit was challenged every day. Remaining under the same roof as someone who was adamant about me vacating, coupled with lawyer visits, inquiries from the children and my decision to remain quiet about the divorce as long as possible, weighed heavy on me.

I'd developed a routine in my day that I felt would best benefit everyone in my environment. Initially, I kept late hours working and sleeping in. This was a coping mechanism that easily became a habit after losing Pinky. With the new Pinky, it became necessary for me to rise earlier to train her and prepare for my new reinvention into a single woman. I decided I would move back to Chicago after the divorce, which meant finding a place to live. It also meant reconnecting with friends and family I'd left over eight-and-a-half years ago, and building a whole new life.

I never imagined I would be a twice-divorced, single woman at forty-two, though my situation was no different from many women who start over in their forties. I knew I wasn't unique, but I also knew I was better equipped than most to get through it, though my emotional well-being would be challenged.

I continued to focus my attention on developing my spirituality. I read books and listened to some of my master mentors online and on YouTube every day (you will learn more about mentors in chapter eight). In addition to spirituality, I'd always been aware of the value of exercise and eating healthy foods. I explored Daoism and through its teachings, became a vegetarian. I consumed myself with nature, took long walks and bicycle rides along the lake with the new Pinky. I spent many hours building my coaching business and fielding inquiries and opportunities for reality TV projects based on my first book, *Undercover Angel.*

Although I was entrenched in a challenging divorce, I was soon able to create a sense of balance in my life. Developing a routine was the only way I knew how to create what I wanted. I exercised daily, ate the healthiest meals I'd ever eaten in my life, enjoyed time in nature, was hyper-focused on my business and discovered other realms of spirituality.

I began to document my days in my journal, knowing one day I would share the healing process with the hope that I could help someone. When I reconnected with my sense of purpose, it became easy to make the shift toward building my future by being present in the *now*. I had days that would take me off this empowering track. I had days filled with tears and disempowering thoughts. I'd ask questions that did not serve me. Why would the universe want me to suffer? What was my part in two failed marriages?

I needed to mourn the end that some psychologists refer to as a form of death, of my relationship and the loss of involvement with my stepchildren. This sadness would rear its head unexpectedly. I focused on what I would miss in the day-to-day activities of the children's lives. The tender moments of having one of my teens sprawl across my lap on the sofa for a back scratch. I'd dearly miss listening to their animated stories about school, their dates, and activities. I was honored to be their confidante, arbitrator and coach in more ways than I can count. I realized my role in their lives and theirs in mine was so sacred that I needed to learn a new way to maintain it the best I could manage even from a distance.

I decided at a very young age that my identity was that of a resilient and flexible person. I set out to find my essence. I applied what I was taught. I told myself it was okay to break down and process whatever showed up in my life. In the midst of one of my dark days, I had an epiphany—I encourage everyone to have a coach, but I was not taking my own advice.

My estranged husband was on the road for business. I was home alone. The children were advised not to visit me during his absence. I was doing some soul searching and began a conversation with God. I asked, "Why would you put me in a position where I get to help raise and love three great children and then have them taken away? Why would you have me meet and marry a man who I devoted my life to only to have the relationship end on a sour note? What did I do to deserve this? What lesson am I supposed to learn? Why is it all crashing down on me? What am I being punished for?"

I loved this family with every ounce of my soul. I freely served my husband and step-kids with all that I had. I felt compelled to have a conversation with someone I'd admired from afar. I reached out to the former wife of one of my mentors. I'd never met her, so I decided to message her on Facebook. Within hours, she responded and graciously offered support in the form of written correspondence and later, phone calls. As cliché as this sounds, when the student is ready, the teacher will appear. That is exactly what happened to me.

Did she give me information that I hadn't already heard? No. What she gave me was something I often give my clients—an opportunity to re-visit a means, a tool or a strategy that they may have overlooked, dismissed or buried. The information is within us and, sometimes, it simply needs an outside party, a coach or mentor, to bring it forth.

New questions began to consume me. What's the best thing I can do for myself in this moment? What gifts had I been given in the relationship when it was healthy? What gifts can I receive from the unhealthy moments in the relationship? As I mentioned before, what we focus on expands, so flooding myself with questions that would serve me permitted me to focus only on answers that would serve me. I am forever grateful for the synchronicity that allowed us to work together during the course of that month.

Remember when I said that I hoped my experience would be a great teacher for someone else one day? That day came less than three months after my divorce.

Tom was an executive I had coached through a painful divorce. After twenty-five years of marriage, his wife inherited a large sum of money, moved out, and filed for divorce. Tom's head was spinning. To add insult to his injury, he discovered his wife was also having an affair. Tom whipped himself into a frenzy of disempowering questions. He was in a state of shock and disbelief when he came to me.

The first thing I recommended to Tom was that he acknowledged and accepted whatever he was feeling in that moment. My goal was not to change his behavior. I needed to understand where he *was*. Initially, I was the listener. Isn't it true that you are more apt to share with someone when they are not trying to solve your problems?

Once I had developed a rapport with Tom, we created a productive plan together to shift his focus. Tom needed to focus on who he was becoming and how he was expanding himself in his new role as a divorced man. He needed to mourn the death of his relationship, and take the time to remember and cherish all that was good in his life and all that came as a result of his relationship.

This is not an easy task in the midst of the divorce. I knew it as much as Tom did. I gave Tom a series of assignments to help him shift his focus, create an action plan, and embrace his reinvention as a divorced man. Time and guided focus are stellar wound healers.

Often we'd become satirical about the situation in order to lighten the mood. Laughter is the quickest way to shift your focus and release a whole bunch of natural, physiological, feel good chemicals, into your body.

Once, I was coaching a client behind closed doors and a family member overheard us laughing hysterically on and off for nearly fifteen minutes. When I completed the session, they asked me who I was talking to. "A client," I responded. They thought it was one of my sisters or best friends!

I manage to have fun with my clients and still yield them tremendous results, quite often utilizing the power of laughter.

DID YOU KNOW?

Laughter is good for your health.

Laughter relaxes the whole body. A good, hearty laugh relieves physical tension and stress, leaving your muscles relaxed for up to forty-five minutes.

Laughter boosts the immune system. Laughter decreases stress hormones and increases immune cells and infection-fighting antibodies, thus improving your resistance to disease.

Laughter triggers the release of endorphins, the body's natural feel-good chemicals. Endorphins promote an overall sense of well-being and can even temporarily relieve pain.

Laughter protects the heart. Laughter improves the function of blood vessels and increases blood flow, which can help protect you against a heart attack and other cardiovascular problems.

I slept and dreamt that life was joy. I awoke and saw that life was service. I acted and behold, service was joy.
—Rabindranath Tagore

Find the Joy

The purpose of life is to experience joy. Our natural state is joy. So why do we sometimes make things so hard for ourselves? Ridding yourself of thoughts of lack, limitation, scarcity, fear, doubt and worry can seem impossible, yet when we choose to fill the gap created by removing those thoughts, there's plenty of room for abundance, joy, love, faith, peace, wisdom, harmony and all things that are good.

Nothing has meaning until we give it meaning. If you decided to label every event as neutral, then good or bad would not exist.

Imagine you are standing at a bus stop after a heavy downpour and a car hits a puddle that splashes water on you from head to toe. To stoke the fire a bit, maybe you were heading to an important meeting or interview and have no time to tidy up. The typical reaction is shock and anger. Not only does it suck to be wet and dirty, but you only get one shot at making a first impression, and now it's ruined.

Negative self-talk begins. *Why me? Why today? I guess I wasn't meant to get the new business or promotion. This has to be a sign that I'm a loser. There's no way I can show up like this! What will they think of me?* You have whipped your emotional state into such a disempowering frenzy by asking yourself poor questions that you've left no room for creative answers and solutions.

Imagine the same scenario with a different reaction. Imagine after being splashed with the puddle that you respond with the question, "Wasn't that exciting?" and started to laugh. Other people around you who witnessed it also began to laugh. Because the emotion of laughter has energetically permeated your space, you decide to be even more comical and ask the observers, "Do you think I still have a chance at the promotion?" Because you chose the state of joy, you begin to notice a series of events start to unfold. Someone offers you tissues to dry yourself. The car responsible pulls over and offers you a ride to your meeting, which gets you to your appointment earlier giving you time to tidy up.

Even if the chain reaction of events did not play out that way, what are you left with? A circumstance that was out of your control that left you in a fit of rage or a fit of laughter.

You are 100% responsible for the emotions you experience. Are you prepared to accept that? I'm not implying that everyone become a Pollyanna. I am strongly suggesting that you hold the ultimate decision about the emotional state you want to hang out in.

Life is 10% what happens to you and 90% how you respond to it. When we decide what we want, how to get there emerges. Joy is the immediate reward for moving toward your mission.

Accept what is out of your control and optimize what is in your control. Make the choice to be your best self, regardless of the circumstances.

If you are a person who enjoys drama and behaves like an alarmist, know that people have you pegged. When they see you coming, they run, hide and will avoid you at all costs. Do you know people like this—complainers, blamers, worriers, hypochondriacs, Debbie Downers? If you are one of them, how do you feel knowing people are merely tolerating you?

Og Mandino says in his book, *The Greatest Salesman in the World*, "Today I will be master of my emotions."

It is important to monitor not only the conversations you have with yourself, but the feelings you experience when you receive news that can take you on a roller coaster ride of negativity.

Look at some of the negative experiences you have had in your life. What good came of them later? I really want you to dig deep for this next exercise. In order for you to prepare for your next reinvention, you must look back and remember the circumstances and experiences that caused you great pain. Reflect on the events that left you feeling disturbed and defeated. The only way for you to break through to the other side is to recall the events you have labeled as failures and defeats.

EXERCISE

List some of the first negative life experiences that come to mind:

Negative Experience:

_____

_____

Lesson Learned:

_____

_____

Negative Experience:

_____

_____

Lesson Learned:

_____

_____

Negative Experience:

_____

_____

Lesson Learned:

_____

_____

A large part of mastering your emotions comes through the use of empowering words. Your words reveal your expectations, so quit talking about doubt. What we talk about most reveals what we expect to happen in our lives and begins to increase the likelihood that it will, whether it is good or not. What happens in our mind begins to happen in our lives.

Whenever you are depressed, angry, anxious or upset, use this as your signal to stop and become aware of your thoughts. Use your feelings as your cue to reflect on your thinking. An effective way to analyze your thoughts is to ask yourself some challenging questions.

THESE QUESTIONS WILL HELP YOU DISCOVER WHETHER YOUR CURRENT OUTLOOK IS VALID:

What is my evidence for and against my thinking?

Are my thoughts factual, or are they just my interpretations?

Am I jumping to negative conclusions?

What else could this mean?

If I were being positive, how would I perceive this event?

Is this situation as bad as I am making out to be?

What is the worst thing that could happen?

What is the best thing that could happen?

What is most likely to happen?

Is there anything good about this situation?

Will this matter in five years?

When you feel anxious, depressed or stressed-out, your conversations with yourself are likely to become extreme. You will be more likely to expect the worst and focus on the most negative aspects of whatever event is happening at that time; therefore, it is helpful to put things into their proper perspective. *Is thinking this way helping me feel good or achieve my goals? What can I do that will help me solve the problem? Is there something I can learn from this situation, to help me do it better next time?*

When you recognize your current way of thinking might be self-defeating, it can sometimes motivate you to look at things from a different point of view.

To start adopting some of these new principles on your quest to master your emotions, you will need to be equipped with a new and improved vocabulary. Certain words need to be deleted completely from your conversations with others and yourself. The words I'm about to share with you have no value in your life. When you catch yourself using these words, replace them with more empowering ones. These new words will help you focus on what's possible instead of feeling hopeless. They will transform your emotions.

Negative Statements Transformed to Positive Statements

NEGATIVE	POSITIVE
I'm annoyed	I'm intrigued
I'm burnt out	I'm recharging my batteries
This is difficult	This is an interesting challenge
I'm afraid	I'm excited
I'm jaded now	This too shall pass
I'm powerless	I'm formulating a solution
I'm overwhelmed	I have many compelling projects
They rejected me	They missed a great opportunity
I got screwed over	I got a great emotional test
Life is hard	Life is full of surprises
People are greedy	Some people operate from scarcity
I'm wiped out	I'm pleasantly spent
I had a horrible day	I had an interesting day
I feel dead tired	I used all of my energy today
I'm sick of work	I'm lucky I have a job
What a hell of a day	What an exciting day
That's impossible	Anything is possible if I'm committed
It's hopeless	I'm hopeful
I can't	I choose not to

Think about the phrases that people at the office and in your family say regularly.

You can't always get what you want.
Life's a bitch.
Accidents happen.
It's hanging over my head.
I'm devastated.
You win some. You lose some.
Life is a game.
Life's tough and then you die.
Win at all costs.
Three strikes and you're out.
That's life.
You never get a break.

We are all influenced by the people in our environment. Which of the metaphors in the previous list of phrases have you adopted? Write them below.

_____

_____

_____

_____

_____

What metaphors do you use that are more useful to your life, values, and beliefs?

Happiness is a day when I wake up.
Love makes the world go around.
Friends are forever.
Love is a journey.
Time is money.
Problems are puzzles.
It's not whether you win or lose. It's how you play the game.

Use the examples above for ideas then write your own in the space below.

_____

_____

_____

_____

People who have great lives think and talk about what they love more than what they don't love. Each day focus on what you love and be sure to monitor your words.

> Stop talking about shortages and setbacks
>
> Stop talking about defeat and disease
>
> Stop talking about failure and problems

Have you ever listened carefully to the words you use and the words other people use in day-to-day communication? A person tells you a great deal about themselves by the words they use. The tone of voice that one uses is very important in how the message will be received, but the exact words share insights you will get nowhere else in the communication experience.

Starting today, pay careful attention to the words and phrases people use that reveal their experience to you.

If I catch myself using a disempowering word or phrase, I immediately rephrase my sentence by replacing it with an empowering word or phrase. When you have access to this new way of thinking, and begin to use it, you will notice your words and phrases more frequently and begin to self-correct unconsciously.

Once you become aware of your own vocabulary and your internal dialogue with yourself, you will become more cognizant of the language and disempowering phrases other people use. You will start to become uncomfortable when you hear them. It is all part of the reinvention process.

Happiness is a conscious choice. It is not an automatic response.

—Rose Barthel

The truth is that our finest moments are most likely to occur when we are feeling deeply uncomfortable, unhappy, or unfulfilled. For it is only in such moments, propelled by our discomfort that we are likely to step out of our ruts and start searching for different ways or truer answers.

—M. Scott Peck

• *Chapter Two* •

WHEN DO WE REINVENT?

*#2 Personal Leverage:
Pain or Pleasure?*

I ntolerance of your present is what creates your future. Each time a major shift happens in your life—leaving a job or a relationship, moving, or losing a loved one—you have to take control of your life or risk never reaching your full potential.

Motivations and emotions may have a purpose related to self-preservation, pain-avoidance and gratification. When you ultimately decide to make a change in your life, you are motivated to do it by leveraging pain or pleasure. The key to motivation is to make the things you want so compelling that it will make you overcome the procrastination, bad habits, limiting beliefs and fears that hold most people back. People are always motivated when there is something they want badly enough.

When I work with clients, my goal is to discover how much leverage they are able to put upon themselves by asking a few questions. When it is revealed that they are motivated by either moving away from pain or by seeking pleasure, I begin the process of associating them with their primary motivating "trigger" or "button".

EXERCISE

To get a sense of your own values, consider for a moment the following questions:

In general, what motivates you?

_____
_____
_____
_____

What inspires you?

_____
_____
_____
_____

What moves you to action?

_____
_____
_____
_____

What gets you out of bed in the morning?

_____
_____
_____
_____

Some possible answers might be:

Success
Praise
Recognition
Love and Acceptance
Something you want (a home, an education, a thinner body,
  a job, a cause)
Making a difference in the world

Most people are motivated by emotional pain (sadness, grief, anger, anxiety). People tend to be motivated by their desire to be rid of emotional pain. As long as pain is there, they are willing to do the work.

People who are more motivated by pleasure (rewarding themselves for accomplishing their goals) usually already have great success in their lives. These people are now simply looking for new ways to enhance their success by giving themselves more cherries on top of their already abundant sundaes.

Nobody changes without pain. Comfort or mediocrity creates longevity.

What if you knew that something you are doing daily was creating disaster or success in your future? Are you ready to do something about it? I'm not trying to glorify emotional pain. I am simply making the point that even negative emotions can be useful. How many people would work to change and improve in the absence of emotional pain? Most would have no motivation to do so.

> *The secret of success is learning how to use pain and pleasure instead of having pain and pleasure use you. If you do that, you're in control of your life. If you don't, life controls you.*
>
> **—Anthony Robbins**

Client Story: Pain or Pleasure

People can become stagnant in their relationships; they have a sense of security, but have lost some of the zest they once had for their partner. A cycle begins. The cycle usually starts with neglecting their health. They stop exercising and gravitate toward unhealthy food choices. They fill their schedules and make excuses as to why it is not convenient to exercise and make better nutritional choices.

When I started coaching Diane, I soon learned that she was twenty-five pounds overweight. Diane had been gaining weight regularly for the past five years and hadn't really given it any thought until she was invited on her husband's company Caribbean cruise that was three months away. Diane knew some of her husband's colleagues and felt immediate anxiety. She was looking forward to an opportunity to rekindle her relationship with her husband in a romantic setting, but was ashamed of her weight.

In order for me to understand how to work with Diane, I needed to find out a few things. I asked her, "What is your ideal weight and why?"

I also asked if she gave her weight any thought at all prior to the cruise. Did her husband pressure her to lose weight or was it her choice? To discover how Diane was going to use leverage on herself, it was imperative that she associated losing weight with her own empowering decision, not societal rules. Otherwise, trying to lose weight would be self-defeating. I knew Diane would not be as committed to keeping the weight off after the big "reveal" on the cruise if she was not completely connected to doing it for herself.

Ultimately, Diane admitted she had gotten into a place of contentment. Knowing that marital partners often go through this pattern, I explained why people opt to disregard their health and exercise habits in exchange for heavier meals and a non-active lifestyle once they've found a life partner. It is as simple as deciding to relax more and indulging in quick, unhealthy food choices because they are in a contented relationship.

Diane agreed. She felt there was no longer any pressure to impress her mate; he was there for the long run and did not seem to mind that extra twenty-five pounds.

I asked Diane if, in her heart of hearts, she was truly happy with her size. She finally came around and said she wasn't. She missed wearing some of her favorite garments and would experience a pang of remorse when she was rifling through her closet and came upon a special item from years past. I asked Diane to take out all of her favorite pieces and hang them in a conspicuous place in her home where she would see them every day. I wanted her to start to feel excitement and joy about those items as she started her new health regimen.

Diane took my advice and went a step further by creating a vision board (you will learn more about this in Chapter 7) that included pictures of some of the clothes she wanted to reward herself with once she reached her goal. This completely changed the way she thought about getting back into shape. Diane's husband also got involved. Not only did he become her cheerleader, he started to adopt some of her habits. He joined her cycling and participated in cooking healthier meals. Diane was able to drop the extra weight and bond with her husband in a new way. Their cycling trips allowed them to feel revitalized and gave them opportunities to enjoy nature and communicate on a different level.

> *When you welcome your emotions as teachers, every*
> *emotion brings good news, even the ones that are painful.*
> **—Gary Zukav**

My Story: Pain or Pleasure

When I began writing my book, *Undercover Angel; From Beauty Queen to SWAT Team,* I hit a slump. It was easy for me to write a chapter about one of my undercover operations or tell a personal story about my experience in the military, but I had trouble weaving the stories together sequentially so the book would flow.

Sharing my personal, feeling side with the business side of my careers was the challenge. I had a friend who was an avid crime reader review several of my chapters. She told me, without pulling any punches that I did not express enough feeling. I had been accustomed to writing police reports and sticking to just the facts, and she thought my book was one massive police report.

I reached out to two of the members in my Masterminds group who were writing books as well. A Masterminds Group is made up of people you choose who have a skill or specialty you can benefit from. The goal is to hold one another accountable to your individual commitments. In this case, we were all committed to writing and finishing our books.

We decided to support each other by proofreading our works. When we realized we could be writing our books for another year—because we were seeking perfection—we decided to place a deadline on the delivery of our books. We set the date for Dec 31, 2006.

We were aware that we needed to gain leverage on ourselves in order to hit our respective goals. After a fun round of banter throwing out ideas for rewards, we realized that the only way we would achieve them was to put our feet to the fire. Our leverage would be to run a marathon. One of the members of the Mastermind group had a bum knee. Asking him to run a marathon equated to tremendous pain. The other member had run a marathon and had vowed never to do it again. I had completed two marathons and felt it was out of my system. Still, our books needed to be finished, so we committed to it by signing a contract with one another—either finish our book by December 31, 2006 or run a marathon.

As with many things in life, setting and achieving goals is not always a straight road. Wouldn't you know it, two days later I received an email from my editor? The editor I had already interviewed and developed a great working relationship with notified me that he would not be able to deliver my completed manuscript until early 2007. I had a choice. Find another editor or run a marathon. I knew I wanted this particular editor to do the work although I really did not want to run a marathon.

Since the military, my word became one of my most valuable assets. I met with my Mastermind group and told them that I would not meet the deadline and thus would be running the marathon. They were awed, though I knew the value of taking immediate responsibility for breaking the contract.

Nothing happens until the pain of remaining the same outweighs the pain of change.
—Arthur Burt

Because it was winter, I decided to run the full 26.2-mile marathon on a treadmill. I don't know anyone who has had the experience of running 26.2 miles on a treadmill, but I can assure you that it was not easy. Just because the running surface was rubber, it didn't make the experience a piece of cake. The scenery didn't change. There weren't crowds of people cheering you along the route, and there was no sense of community with other runners to inspire you.

My stepchildren did rally around me intermittently for the several hours it took to complete the goal. Do you think that made an impression on them about keeping one's word? In the end, we *all* realized the power of commitment and a Mastermind group.

I hope you are able to see how getting leverage on yourself is the best way to achieve a goal. Can you think of a time where you used either the carrot or the stick strategy as leverage to achieve a goal?

> *It is by going down into the abyss that we recover the treasures of life. Where you stumble, there lies your treasure.*
> **—Joseph Campbell**

Let me elaborate how to use pain as leverage by following this six part sequence to determine how pain can be used for motivation. After coaching thousands of people over the years, I learned the most common stopping block preventing people from achieving a goal is procrastination so I will use procrastination in the following example. You can use this formula with any habit you are looking to change.

1. **Associate pain to the behavior you don't want**
   When I catch myself procrastinating, I must immediately announce on one of my social networking sites that I let myself down by doing this (explain what derailed you) instead of committing to my goal.
2. **Interrupt the pattern of the behavior**
   Now go and post.
3. **Create leverage and assign a new empowering behavior**
   After the post sits for thirty minutes, go back and repost that you have recommitted to your goal.
4. **Associate pleasure to the new empowering behavior**
   Because you have recommitted, forgive yourself. Truly let go and take immediate action toward your original goal.
5. **Anchor the new behavior into your nervous system**
   Put on some great, uplifting music and journal about your accomplishment of recommitting place your hand on your heart and announce it out loud.
6. **Create a plan of action that supports your new behavior**
   Commit to following this formula every time you procrastinate.

EXERCISE

Develop Better Habits

Did you know it takes thirty consecutive days to create a consistent habit? It only takes three or four outstanding habits to create a phenomenal life.

When you want something you have never had, you have to do something you have never done! Answer the following questions as completely as possible.

What are the five habits you need to change? Add your start date.

_____
_____
_____
_____
_____

What will changing these give you?

_____
_____
_____
_____
_____

What are your five greatest habits currently?

_____
_____
_____
_____
_____

What are five new habits you'd like to implement immediately? Add your start date.

_____

_____

_____

_____

_____

> There are two basic motivating forces: fear and love. When we are afraid, we pull back from life. When we are in love, we open to all that life has to offer with passion, excitement, and acceptance. We need to learn to love ourselves first, in all our glory and our imperfections. If we cannot love ourselves, we cannot fully open to our ability to love others or our potential to create. Evolution and all hopes for a better world rest in the fearlessness and openhearted vision of people who embrace life.
> **—John Lennon**

If your actions inspire others to dream more, learn more, do more and become more, you are a leader.

—John Quincy Adams

• *Chapter Three* •

YOUR PATH

*#3 Six Tips to Breakthrough
to the New YOU*

I shared these tips during my appearance on *The Big Idea with Donny Deutsch* after the release of my first book, *Undercover Angel: From Beauty Queen to SWAT Team* in 2007, after reflecting on the tools that had yielded the most rewards in my life. I have not invented any new schools of thought with these six tips. They are simply the guidelines I used repeatedly to get positive results in my life. After reviewing these tips, you will have an opportunity to see how they relate to accomplishments you have experienced in your own life.

> *From SWAT Team to Reinvention Life Coach to author of Undercover Angel, if she doesn't get YOU to go all in, I don't know who is going to do it"*
> **—Donny Deutsch**

Take Uncalculated Risks

> *Twenty years from now, you will be more disappointed by the things that you didn't do than by the ones you did. So throw off the bowlines. Sail away from the safe harbor. Catch the trade winds in your sails. Explore. Dream. Discover.*
> **—Mark Twain**

FROM UNDERCOVER ANGEL

Alas, the life of parading in crowns and gowns was once my naive reality. I was born fifth into a family of seven children, and we were living at poverty level. Although we were on welfare, and Dad always seemed to be working around the clock, it was never enough. I just graduated high school and enrolled in Daley Community College. This would make me the first member of my family to attend college. I didn't care that it was an hour commute, and I had to take three city buses to get there. I continued waitressing full time at a local restaurant with hopes of saving enough money to attend a state university for my second year.

In mid-June, I answered a telephone call from Veronica Reed, an official with the Miss Illinois-USA Pageant. "I'm calling to tell you congratulations. You have been accepted to compete in the pageant." My heart pounded. Confused, all I could muster was "Thank you." I continued listening in a haze as she rambled on about sponsors, applications, and deadlines before congratulating me again and hanging up.

I raced into the basement where Mom was folding laundry and said, "Mom, I just hung up with someone from the Miss Illinois pageant and she said I've been accepted to compete." She exclaimed, "Really!" and hugged me tightly into her robust Italian frame. "Mom, what did you do, how did this happen?" She smiled wryly and said, "I came across an application, filled it out and sent a picture of you." This was the greatest surprise of my life.

As an idyllic escape from our meager lifestyle, our family frequently watched the various pageants on television throughout the year and always rooted for Miss Illinois. I secretly dreamed of competing in a pageant, but thought of myself as too short. A year earlier, Mom had taken me to a finishing school to inquire about the cost of enrollment. A staff member had bluntly told us that, at 5'5", I was not tall enough to be considered for any kind of fashion or modeling work. We naively took that information as sacred and banished any further thoughts of a modeling career. Mom, however, had the final card hidden up her sleeve.

I soon found out that the pageantry business was just that—a business. Each contestant was required to pay a $1500 entry fee, as well as purchase an evening gown, a business suit for arrival and interview day, a swimsuit, and special workout clothing for the opening number rehearsals. They may as well have told me that I needed to win the lottery first. We had no idea where I was going to get that kind of money until we found out that the pageant encouraged soliciting sponsorships to defray the cost.

My resourceful Mom took out an ad in the local newspaper requesting that businesses contact her if they were interested in supporting their "very own" south side girl. The ad worked. The next few months made for a thrilling ride. I joined a health club and practiced walking in high heels. As Mom and I shopped together, I listened to her boast to the store clerks that her daughter was competing in the Miss Illinois pageant. I felt like a celebrity trying on evening gowns and swimsuits.

A whole new world was opening up for this dark blonde 110 lb, 5'5" brown-eyed eighteen-year-old girl. The one striking physical quality that I was often recognized for was my prominently high cheekbones. I received these from Dad's gene pool. His parents were a mixture of Swedish, English and Native American Indian (Cherokee).

Mid-fall, Mom and Dad dropped me off at the venue to prepare for the three-day pageant event. I was awestruck as I was shuttled between various registration points with the other 204 contestants from across Illinois. Many of the women exuded refinement and wealth, as indicated by their Louis Vuitton luggage and "to die for" business ensembles. This made me question my acceptance into the pageant. Beauty, poise and personality were the only requirements for competing and I thought I possessed all of them, but was suddenly feeling less than adequate. Who was I anyway? I was eighteen, living at home, attending a community college and working as a waitress. Was this the making of a Miss Illinois winner?

When I arrived in my hotel room and began unpacking, this gorgeous, classy blonde entered the room. With a flawless smile and whirlwind appeal, she introduced herself as my "roomie" Diane," told me my suit was dynamite, and offered to change beds if I preferred to sleep near the window. Feeling clumsy and timid, I mustered, "No, I'm fine." Surely, the jig was up. She probably thought I could have used some classes on etiquette to communicate on her level. She asked to see my evening gown and responded with the same "dynamite" exclamation. I admired her confidence and style, and thought I was lucky to have her as a roommate. At bedtime, we spent a little time with "getting to know you" questions, and I learned that my refined and flawless roomie was the former Miss Teen-Illinois. Of course she was.

We arose ninety minutes before our scheduled group breakfast to primp for our official debut with the pageant officials. Diane's toiletry supplies made the sink look like a department store cosmetic counter. What was all that stuff? I had all of two hair products (shampoo and hairspray) and the bare essentials for my face.

At breakfast the cliques were already forming. Diane instantly began hobnobbing with the pageant officials, who welcomed her with hugs. I continued to watch and learn, as my fellow contestants resumed their endless primping. I was an "apply-the-lipstick-once-and-forget-about-it-for-the-rest- of-the-night" kind of girl. These women were constantly whipping out mini- compact mirrors and touching up their canvases.

At orientation, I spotted a woman who could have easily passed for Christie Brinkley's little sister. She had flawless skin, baby blue eyes, hair that resembled Farrah Fawcett's from her famed poster, and she stood six feet in height. Her stunning beauty mesmerized me; I would have guessed that she was already a professional model for the likes of Cover Girl. I continued scanning the room, comparing myself to other girls, hoping to find less competition. I was so incredibly naive. What did winning Miss Illinois really mean? The only thing I knew for certain was the prizes that the title winner would receive—scholarship money and miscellaneous perks. The scholarship money was the reason I was there.

After orientation, we began rehearsing the opening dance number. I had never taken a dance class in my life, and it showed. The experienced women were given the prime spots on stage, performing quick jazzy numbers, while the challenged women, like me, were thrown into two long chorus lines. Beauty, poise and personality—I think not. It was becoming increasingly clear who belonged in the winner's circle.

At bedtime, my roomie asked where I had trained to walk a runway. Trained to walk a runway? Was she joking? Boy was I out of my league! I responded, "I never trained, it looks simple enough," trying to convince both of us. Initially, she stared at me in disbelief, and then her wide eyes softened to a look of reassurance. She must have felt sympathy, because she added, "I'll teach you tomorrow if you like." How was I supposed to learn all of this stuff in two days, when some women had spent their entire lives preparing for this one opportunity?

Half of the following day was spent rehearsing our dance number and the other half was spent on oral interviews. The ten interviewers sat behind long tables. Surely, these women had interview coaches and had prepped diligently before today. There was nothing I could do now except feign confidence.

When our leg of girls was called into the room, I took note of the demeanor of the girls who'd just finished. They exited tight-lipped and professional. I followed my roomie and looked to her for guidance as we were directed around the table. When the conductor called out the official start time and sounded a buzzer, I seated myself in front of a woman. As she kept her head buried in a file, I was horrified when I noticed Diane still standing behind her chair, waiting to be invited to take a seat. When she was acknowledged, she extended her hand and smartly introduced herself before sitting. Too late for me, I was instantly mortified at my obvious lack of etiquette and forced a smile as my interviewer introduced herself.

Is attending a State University really that important to me? I pondered as I considered disappearing under the table for the next two days. The interviewer asked, "Are you nervous?" I replied, "Yes...a little." She suggested I take a deep breath and relax. As I put each interviewer under my belt, my confidence soared.

The next day consisted of more tedious rehearsal; minutes before our first walk I could feel the butterflies fluttering in my stomach. Our dance number started, and the first talented group of girls marched onstage to a roar of applause and high-pitched whistles. I made my grand debut as part of the chorus line halfway through the song. I knew my family must have been eagerly trying to spot me; with no formal dance experience, they couldn't have been too surprised to see me arrive in a line of talentless high kickers.

We hustled off stage in a frenzy, tearing through the dressing room to change into our swimsuits. Again, the mirror mob scene was reenacted. Girls assisted other girls with taping their breasts together and fastening their swimsuit bottoms to their bums.

Soon after, the mayhem backstage was repeated. New hairstyles were needed for the evening gown competition. Blow dryers, rollers and curling irons were running full force. Half-naked women with taped breasts pranced about as mini-emergencies erupted.

My evening gown was dazzling: a form-fitting, full-length, black sequined gown with gold, flame-like sequins framing the plunging neckline and shoulders. A pair of black-patent-leather shoes with gold flames complemented the gown. Feeling the weight of the gown on my body as I walked made me feel as rich and as beautiful as Crystal on Dynasty. Again, I took the stage and walked with exaggerated poise and elegance, making eye contact with the sea of judges in the first row.

I arose the next morning feeling different. The evening before was thrilling, yet I felt a sense of peace on this new day because I took myself out of the equation. I knew I didn't meet the standards of what they were looking for in the winner. The other ladies however, appeared exceptionally nervous. The cliques gathered and opinions were offered on who would make the final cut. I, too, had my ten finalists in mind. As all 205 of us filled the rear of the stage, the ten names were called. The usual shrieks of excitement followed, and the remainder of us poured off stage.

The dressing room felt like a graveside funeral. As I peered around the room, I felt removed from it all. Women were weeping and consoling one another. I realized why I felt less affected—most of these women had centered their lives on the outcome of this event. I never made any conscious effort to compete; after all, it was Mom who entered me and I spent less than four months preparing for it.

I joined my family members—who all gave me real Italian hugs this time— and rooted for the Christie Brinkley look-alike I'd spotted the first day. My top pick, the gorgeous, six-foot, Purdue University senior became Miss Illinois-USA. She went on to make the top ten finalists for the country in the Miss USA pageant.

EXERCISE

In order to succeed, you need to make it *a must* to leave your perceived comfort zones.

What would immediately happen if you stepped out of your comfort zone?

_____

_____

_____

_____

_____

_____

_____

_____

_____

_____

_____

_____

_____

_____

_____

_____

_____

_____

_____

_____

_____

_____

_____

Say "Yes" Before Your Brain Can Say "No"

> *The person who really wants to do something finds a*
> *way; the other person finds an excuse.*
> **—Author Unknown**

Don't wait until conditions are perfect. If you are waiting to start until conditions are perfect, you probably never will. There will always be something that isn't quite right. Either the timing is off, or there is too much competition. In the real world, there is no perfect time to start. You have to take action and deal with problems as they arise.

Be a doer and practice doing things every day rather than thinking about them. Do you want to start exercising? Do you have a great new idea business idea? Do it today. The longer an idea sits in your head without being acted on, the weaker it becomes. After a few days, the details get hazy. After a week, it's forgotten completely. By becoming a doer, you will get more done and stimulate new ideas in the process.

FROM UNDERCOVER ANGEL

Shortly after the pageant, I researched all of the branches of the military, discovered that the Air Force seemed to offer the best package, and would finance four years of University. My choice was made; now I just needed to convince Mom that it was the right one.

At the U.S. Air Force recruiter's office I was met by a well-built man who took one look at this smartly dressed (I wore my pageant business suit; it was the only professional thing I owned), petite woman before him and practically dismissed me. With the little grooming and interview etiquette tips I'd picked up from the pageant experience, I believe the sergeant thought he'd been set up for a joke. "Yes, I'm seriously interested in enlisting." After shaking off his initial shock he said, "Have a seat." He composed himself and supplied me with study materials and test dates. I walked out of the recruiter's door knowing that this was the right thing to do.

Breaking the news to my parents was my next challenge. Mom was appalled. "Do you realize that you can be sent to fight in a war?" she said as Dad looked on. "Yes Mom, but the probability of that is pretty low." Continuing, I pleaded, "Mom this is the only way I know how to pay for four years of college, and that's the most important thing to me right now." I opened some of the Air Force brochures that showed pictures of young, sharply dressed military men and women engaged in different career fields smiling and appearing fit and intelligent. She rifled through some of it, appearing increasingly interested, and asked, "What if you hate it...will they let you out?"

"Well...no, Mom, when I enlist, I sign a contract for four years."

Dad surprisingly perked up. "I tried to get in the Air Force before I met your mother...I didn't pass the test." That was quite the disclosure. Not the fact that he didn't pass; Dad dropped out of high school in the ninth grade. I was astonished that he was interested in becoming a soldier in the very branch I was going to enlist. Mom didn't say much else and Dad, who used up his word quota of the day, continued looking through the paperwork.

So my decision was made. Little did I know what a bond this would create between Dad and I. As I studied the ASVAB (Armed Services Vocational Aptitude Battery) study guide to prepare for the entrance exam, I came across a section in the mechanical field for which I knew nothing about. How on earth did they expect an eighteen-year-old girl to know about the inner working of a car's engine? Or have knowledge about the polarity of electricity? Yuck! It was bad enough helping around the house with yard work; the last thing I wanted to do was dive under the hood of some smelly car and get grease under my fingernails changing a broken spark plug. Sitting at the kitchen table, I asked Dad, "What's a spark plug?" Dad looked at me quizzically, never expecting to hear that sort of question from his delicate daughter, and answered, "It ignites the fuel in the engine on the car. Why?"

This one question awakened Dad's desire to see that his daughter would pass the exam. He escorted me out to his car and began the tedious job of teaching me the inner workings of an engine. I brought out a note pad and diligently drew diagrams and took notes. At times, I could tell I tested his patience.

"Why is everything so greasy under here?" I asked.

"Because it's an engine," he snapped.

I pressed on, "Can't you clean it, like hose it down or something?"

I'm sure at that point, he wondered if his efforts were futile.

Over the next few days, I asked him to read off the prep questions and test my knowledge. One area I have always been gifted is my ability to learn new information and spew it back in record time. Dad was impressed, and I realized that this was the first time I ever asked him to help me study for anything.

Weeks later, I aced the exam scoring high in the mechanical field. So high in fact, my recruiter persuaded me to sign up for a job in that field. He convinced me that the military was short on women in that area and the probability of promotion was high.

Later, I realized the recruiter's main job is to enlist as many naïve kids as possible and fill in the gaps where there are shortages. The last thing they're concerned about is whether or not you're the perfect fit for the job. I saw myself doing something administrative (the area where I scored the highest) but foolishly believed that the recruiter was looking out for my best interests.

Because I still didn't want to get grease under my fingernails I chose what I thought would be the cleanest mechanical job there was: airframe body mechanic. The recruiter explained that I could put in for that job but there was no guarantee I would get it. The only guarantee the military could make was that I would get one of my top three choices for desired regions to be stationed. I was clueless.

Think of three times in your life when you took action, saying yes to something even though you were fearful, and ended up having a great result. Write the event and the outcome.

Event

_____

_____

Outcome

_____

_____

Event

_____

_____

Outcome

_____

_____

Event

_____

_____

Outcome

_____

_____

"Act as if" You've Done it Before

> *You must be the person you have never had the courage to be. Gradually, you will discover that you are that person, but until you can see this clearly, you must pretend and invent.*
>
> **—Paulo Coelho**

The "act-as-if" principle says we can create our circumstances by acting "as if" they are already real. For example, we can be happy by simply acting as if we are happy. While the principle might seem to be based on superficial, "magical" reasoning, it does have some validity when it is used with regular practice. How you view yourself is how others will see you and treat you. So why not choose to act like a hero?

When I was eleven years old, I was devastated when my father was laid off as a janitor at City Hall in Chicago. My father, a high school dropout, was always juggling jobs to help support our family of nine with welfare supplementing his poverty level income. Often our family was put on a charity list to receive food at Thanksgiving and Christmas. It was 1980 when my father landed a job as a parking lot attendant on a small parcel of land in downtown Chicago.

Somehow, I convinced my father to allow me to join him at work during the bitter cold days of my Christmas school break. The parking lot was on Wabash, a notorious Chicago street just under the steel beams of the noisy El-train tracks. The parking lot sat between two buildings and had a maximum capacity of forty vehicles. Next to one of the buildings sat a tiny wooden shanty house—dad's office. Inside the office were his meager furnishings consisting of a tall swivel chair, portable heater, a makeshift desk to keep track of paperwork, and a punch clock.

I'd watch him run to and from the warmth of the shanty, parking vehicles of rich Chicago business people who were paying upwards of $15k for annual parking. Dad was lucky to make $40 in tips after a twelve hour shift to supplement his minimum wages. As I watched him scurry through the lot, shuffling and arranging the vehicles, it broke my heart. He'd return to the shanty with his nose running. I'd hand him a tissue, watching him warm his frozen hands and wind burned face in front of the electric heater.

LISA LOCKWOOD | 59

I'd look for ways to make him feel important by asking how he knew how to drive so many different kinds of cars or how many cars he drove in a week or his favorite car to drive.

I tell you this story for one reason—this is the first time I remember using one of the six life principles I'm sharing with you.

I acted *as if*. At a very young age, in that moment, I felt responsible for salvaging Dad's pride by making his job seem important. I did this by repressing my own pain and discomfort and forcing myself to turn it into something empowering for both of us. Would it have been useful for my father to see me crying, which is what I really felt like doing? I enjoyed my day with my Dad and felt a bit more mature after that experience. The *acting as if* skill had been developed. I used it over and over again to get great results in my life.

Acting as if is synonymous with *fake it until you make it* although it is not about faking happiness until you trick yourself into being happy. It's not about acting like you are cool until other people believe you are and then basing your life around a made-up personality. It's about confidence. It's about meeting situations you feel intimidated by head-on and telling yourself that you are ready for them. It's about putting I-can-do-this intentions out there until you have done such a good job convincing yourself that you suddenly can handle the challenges before you.

Fast-forward fifteen years. I was now a police officer and was asked by the internet sex-crime prevention detective to pose as a fourteen-year-old girl via telephone. I was twenty-eight years old and needed to convince a child sex-predator that I was a fourteen-year-old girl named Missy. Talk about daunting. First, I said yes before my brain could say no and then I went into action.

I reflected on what was important to a fourteen-year-old. Fortunately, I had a few nieces that age that I used as references to get into character before the call. In a locked office with a tape recorder and an FBI agent overseeing the operation, I answered the phone in character and convinced the sex-predator I was fourteen. An arrest followed, and I realized once again that *acting as if* can yield incredible results.

EXERCISE

Write down a time in your life when you acted as if you were someone else or had the skill of someone else and had a rewarding experience as a result.

_____

_____

_____

_____

_____

_____

_____

_____

_____

_____

_____

_____

_____

_____

_____

_____

_____

_____

_____

_____

_____

_____

_____

Become Thick-Skinned

Care about what other people think and you will always be their prisoner.

—Lao Tzu

It's important to understand that people's actions, even when hurtful, rarely have anything to do with you. It's easy to read into the negativity of others and see it as a slight to your personality or challenge to your ego. This type of reaction can trigger unnecessary stress and prevent you from focusing on the positive things in your life. People are people; there is never a need to link their behavior and your happiness. Knowing this gives you freedom to feel the confidence you deserve.

How would your life be different if you stopped allowing other people to dilute or poison your day with their words or opinions? How do you not become offended when someone judges, insults or spreads unkind, untrue rumors? It's not easy. Like any skill in life, it is a skill that requires a continuous effort in order for it to develop into an unconscious habit. Like building muscles, building habits requires repetition. Becoming thick skinned or wearing my coat of armor has become an extremely useful skill. Especially when what I really want to do, in some situations, is curl up in bed under a blanket and disappear forever. Once you develop this skill, you will become a force to be reckoned with.

No one can make you feel inferior without your consent.

—Eleanor Roosevelt

FROM UNDERCOVER ANGEL

My reception as a dispatcher wasn't as welcomed as I thought it would be. The gossip in the radio room (dispatch center) was so cutting that it was difficult to function. I learned from Mark, the only male dispatcher in the department and one of my assigned trainers, that it was common to be given the cold shoulder by the women. I was fresh meat and, as he put it, "It doesn't help that you're thin and attractive." Some of the other women dispatchers had either dated, were married-to, or longed to date the police officers.

Mark and I clicked instantly when we learned that we shared the same sense of humor. He would often have the ladies in stitches with his impersonations of some of his ridiculous 911 calls. Extremely intelligent, he juggled his dispatch job, law school, and a part-time police officer position with apparent ease. On top of this, he was a musician in a local band. Aside from that, he was my most challenging trainer. I received a pass status and was deemed to be ready by Mark after the standard three months of training.

I was confident and ready to handle my own dispatch computer system when I was called into a meeting with the dispatch center supervisor. "Have a seat Lisa," she said, wearing a strained smile. This was the official moment when she would release me from training and assign me to midnight shift. I was thrilled. However, she looked uncomfortable, fidgeting with paperwork as she continued. "There have been some rumors that have even made it to the Chief, that you are having an affair with Mark." "What!" I exclaimed incredulously.

"Several people have brought it to my attention that you too have gotten very close during your training and I have to take some action based on that," she said matter-of-factly.

Horrified, I replied, "I have no idea why someone would say something like that, but I can assure you, it's not true!" "I spoke to the Chief and because of this I decided to put you back in training with another dispatcher to ensure you're equipped to handle the job." Infuriated at the accusation, I said, "So let me get this straight. If someone starts a rumor, it's assumed to be true, and I am punished for it?" "Lisa," she said, sounding exasperated, "it's the only way for me to prove you weren't given passing grades that you didn't deserve."

I knew that some of the women in dispatch were threatened by me physically, and Mark warned me that appearing at work smiling and confident fed their jealousy. I never fathomed it would reach this level. I walked out of her office feeling as if I had a dagger lodged into my back and drove home feeling paralyzed.

After reflecting on the situation further, I decided that I'd show those backstabbers I can do the job and their little stunt will have no effect on me. I vowed to show up at work looking even more cheerful than before. I consulted with Mark, who was equally livid. He said, "I knew they were vicious but didn't expect this." He also chose the same solution that was to behave as if he were unaffected.

I kept my word. On my first day back and each day thereafter, I arrived for work wearing my happy mask. When some of the busybodies asked about my re-

training, I simply said, "Ask the dispatch supervisor." After an additional month of training with one of the senior female dispatchers in the department—who incidentally was one of the few who didn't have seem to hate me—I was cleared to work independently. I'd won!

The bottom line and important lesson here is to stop being offended! See your enemy as your benefactor. They are your greatest emotional trainers. Practice gratitude toward everyone who touches your life and for everything that happens to you.

FOUR IMPORTANT REMINDERS FOR DEVELOPING A THICK SKIN

Only listen to what a critic is saying if you respect them.

Don't be defensive—you feed a critic's fire by firing back.

Delay your reaction. Remove yourself from the scenario and refrain from addressing it verbally or in writing until your heightened emotion has dissipated.

Don't expect everyone to understand your journey especially if they've never had to walk your path.

EXERCISE

Here's your opportunity to write about a time in your life when you needed to put on a thick skin and then achieved a great result.

_____
_____
_____
_____
_____
_____
_____
_____
_____
_____
_____
_____
_____
_____
_____
_____
_____
_____
_____
_____
_____
_____

Go Against the Current

> *Today I will do what others won't, so tomorrow I can*
> *accomplish what others can't.*
>
> **—Jerry Rice**

It's been said that the people who go against the current yield the greatest rewards. Here's an example of just that:

FROM UNDERCOVER ANGEL

Unfortunately, the events surrounding the SWAT selection were preceded by more drama than I was prepared for. One applicant, Officer LaRosa, was an expert marksman and was also a firearms instructor. LaRosa had many qualifications for the position. It just seemed that he was more focused on guns and shooting than actually hitting the street and arresting criminals.

LaRosa was up against three other applicants, myself (a twenty-six month military veteran and a woman), Officer Sharkey and Officer Dudley (who did not officially qualify for the position because of his lack of tenure) and considered himself a shoe-in. Then rumors began to surface about my being the favorite due to my ability to be a team player, my aggressiveness on patrol and overall dedication to the department, which made LaRosa angry. So angry in fact, he began to spread his own rumors. A few of my colleagues shared this information with me and I felt my only recourse was to confront LaRosa.

During patrol, I contacted LaRosa over our squad car computer and requested we meet for a chat and he agreed. I told him point blank, "I've been hearing rumors that I was the favorite for the SWAT position and numerous people in the department have approached me and told me you have been saying that I'm only being considered because of my breasts and blonde hair." He looked at me smugly and replied, "Yeah, I said that."

Pissed off at his arrogance, I asked, "Do you really believe that's the reason why I am 'allegedly' being considered over you?"

He responded, "I don't know, maybe they want a woman on the team. I know Selleck has a 'thing' for you."

"Oh really? There are probably fifty cops that would say Selleck has a 'thing' for you," I shot back. It was a well-known fact in the department that Commander Selleck had an affinity toward LaRosa because of their similar shooting interests.

LaRosa laughed at the comment.

Knowing it was true. I continued, "I don't know who they're going to choose for the position, but I want you to know if they do choose you, that you won't hear me spreading ugly rumors about why you were selected."

LaRosa finished by saying, "Sorry I said that shit, but if they do pick you, I want you to know I think they made the wrong decision."

"You're entitled to that," I replied before driving off.

The nerve of that guy I thought. It was common knowledge that LaRosa was not a go-getter, had low arrest stats, yet wouldn't allow himself to look at me as an equal, based on my gender and appearance. Guys in the department made side bets about who would get the promotion. A few of my "friends" would secretly relay to me what was being said, things like "Lockwood's a shoe-in. She's been licking Charlie's boots since she started." "LaRosa's got it all the way, he's Charlie's gun-bitch." "SWAT is never gonna put a woman on the team, some members have already said they're leaving the team if Lockwood gets on." "The guys are worried she'll file sexual harassment charges if they say 'fuck' in front of her."

I expected some slack from the men, but still felt hurt and betrayed. I'd been helping them train, socialized at lunch with them and even took off into the woods to relieve myself, trying to fit in. I was okay as their role player, but that was it. All they knew was an all-male team, and that's exactly how they wanted to keep it. I knew the team leaders were looking for a levelheaded team player who had proven themselves effective through proactive police activity and dedication to the department. It was the team members that wanted to keep it a boy's club. As much as I wanted to believe the guys would perceive me as an equal, the reality was that it wasn't going to happen. If I was selected, it would be like starting all over again, yet another time for me to prove myself in a man's world.

Weeks later, on my day off, Selleck phoned me at home and said, "Feel like celebrating tonight?" "Why?" "I figured a new SWAT member would want to celebrate." My heart raced. "Oh my God, thank you Commander!" "Don't thank me, you earned it and the panel believed you deserved it." So, after all was said and done, I proved to be the person they were looking for and became the first woman on the SWAT team.

EXERCISE

Have you ever beat your drum in spite of the odds against you? Share an event from your past when you did just that. How did you feel before and after having "gone for it?"

Event

_____

_____

_____

_____

_____

_____

How you felt before

_____

_____

_____

_____

_____

How you felt after

_____

_____

_____

_____

Live Extreme

It takes courage to live as your authentic self. Some people, even family members, may not want to accept the real you. However, if you don't live that way, you become less of yourself and less to those around you. Walking to the beat of your own drum allows you to use all your gifts and be there for others. Every choice you make contains the choice to be authentic.

> *A hero is an ordinary individual who finds strength*
> *to persevere and endure in spite of overwhelming obstacles.*
> **—Christopher Reeve**

Courage is discovering you may or may not win and still trying when you know you might lose. Continually ask yourself, "What can I do, in this moment, to keep moving forward?"

FROM UNDERCOVER ANGEL

Nuzzled fireside on my cocoon-like futon, writing my list of goals and dreams for 2003 was no different from past Januarys. I had asked myself repeatedly over the last year, if money were abundant, what would I love to do in this life? After attending a series of life-balancing seminars in 2001 and 2002, I was beginning to get a clearer picture of what I truly wanted from my life. I wanted to travel the world helping people. I felt so comfortable offering a kind ear, giving advice, and opening the eyes of family, friends and colleagues. People took notice of how I was able to form associations with people from all walks of life. I even had my share of arrestees and informants tracking me down, seeking a connection, and often trumping up some unlikely cover story in order to speak with me.

One man, whom Bosley and I put away for seven years said, "The first thing I'm gonna do when I get out of jail is marry Lockwood." After seven years of law enforcement, I felt I had truly fulfilled all my police desires for excitement, challenge and growth. Many of my superiors and colleagues assumed that I would become a sergeant and even foresaw the chief's position in my distant future. One officer planted a copy of The Police Chief magazine in my mailbox and superimposed my head on the front cover.

So many people could not understand why I wasn't interested in becoming a sergeant. I remember meeting Officer Hull for coffee on midnight shift before one of the sergeant's exams. At the time, I was a three-and-a-half year

*veteran and had the specialties of Juvenile Officer, Firearms Instructor, and
member of SWAT.*

Hull asked, "So, have you been studying for the police exam?"

"I'm not taking the exam."

"Bullshit! They have you pegged as the first female sergeant."

"Well, I'm not sure how that is going to happen if I don't take the test."

"You're so full of it Lockwood, you're gonna be like one of those sleepers that
says they're not taking the test and is secretly studying every minute of the day."

"You'll see," I said, giggling.

"Okay, maybe you don't plan on taking this test, but I guarantee you become
sergeant on this department."

"Wanna bet?"

"Yeah, I get five hundred bucks the day you get promoted."

"And I get five hundred bucks if I retire or resign?"

"You're only taking the bet to camouflage your intentions; it's all part of your
master plan to throw us off your trail. Besides, five hundred bucks ain't nothin'
after you get your salary increase."

Again, I laughed and offered my hand to shake on our deal.

It's peculiar to me even now that I knew I didn't want to become a sergeant. It
was early in my career and like most rookies, I wanted the variety and excitement
that patrol and tactical units offered. The duties of a sergeant—running the
street, ensuring officers remained in their beats, proofreading officer's reports and
disciplining the wayward boys for various infractions—did not seem enticing. I
also figured that I had plenty of time to think about that decision later in my
career, after I've had years of experience on SWAT and in the detective unit.

Time had flown since my meeting with Hull. I was in flux. Bosley and I
were finishing the last leg of our three-year assignment as Narcotic Detectives. My
choices were to leave Narcotics and be promoted to sergeant (provided I aced the
exams and interviews), go back to patrol, or go for a lateral transfer as a general
case detective. But none of those options was compelling. Becoming a general case
detective translated to paper and financial crimes. It was the complete opposite of
what I was currently doing, and I couldn't imagine spending long hours at a desk
or processing crime scenes.

Returning to the street as a uniformed patrol officer offered variety and
challenge, but I perceived the uniform and the restrictions of assigned beats as a
loss of freedom.

Without knowing exactly how I was going to generate income commensurate with my lifestyle, I secretly set my resignation date for December 31st, 2003. That gave me one year to find my dream career. I went through the motions of preparing for the sergeant's exam. I thought I owed it to everyone who had helped my career to take the test.

Hours passed as I continued writing my 2003 goals. Then I was paged—I was to report immediately to assist the detective unit serving an arrest warrant on an armed robber. I jolted from my cozy nook and bundled up to prepare for surveillance on the frigid winter evening. One more year, I lamented. Could I really leave law enforcement?

I gave my thirty days resignation notice to the department. The Chief summoned me into his office to explain my unexpected departure. After listening to my incessant gushing for fifteen minutes and sharing that I would be moving to Montreal and writing a book, he said, "Well I can't compete with that." He thanked me for my years of service and dedication to the department and told me I would be greatly missed. Word had spread about my resignation and I was approached by everyone from the custodian (Corey, my special friend) to judges, bailiffs and clerks from the courthouse, all wishing me well.

On May 7, 2003, one day after my seven-year anniversary as a police officer, I left behind SWAT member, Narcotics Detective and Officer of the Year. I handed in my gun and badge and turned the page from one of the most rewarding, exciting, challenging—and dangerous—chapters of my life.

EXERCISE

Think of a time in your life when you took your biggest leap of faith, when you felt courageous, alive, and empowered. Write about it in the space below

Leap of Faith Event

_____
_____
_____
_____

How did you feel just before you took action?

_____
_____
_____
_____

How did you feel during event?

_____
_____
_____
_____

How did you feel after having accomplished it?

_____
_____
_____
_____

71

*God's gift to me is more talent and ability than I can
possibly use in my lifetime. My gift to God is to develop as
much of that talent and ability as I can in this lifetime.*

—Wallace Wattles

Chapter Four

YOUR MISSION

#4 Discovering Your Life Mission

*S*elfless contribution equals true fulfillment! The question is not what I can do for a living, but rather what would I *love* to do for a living, Gary Zukav writes in *The Seat of the Soul*.

You will never leave where you are until you determine where you want to be. Many people hate where they are, but they don't have a picture of where they want to go. An undefined goal and vagueness will exhaust you. On your quest to discover your life mission, it is important to be in the best possible emotional state, given your current situation.

If you're unemployed, you'll have much more time to shape and structure your plan of action. If you're employed, your mission is to make the best of your current condition while you are planning your next reinvention. It doesn't matter if you loathe your current job. You must find a creative solution to making the best of it until you can move on, and you must take steps to make it happen.

Trust me, I can relate to job dissatisfaction.

FROM UNDERCOVER ANGEL

After three months, my training on the larger vehicles had ceased. A roster was posted in the dispatch center so all of the airmen knew what their daily duties entailed. More times than not I was assigned to the wash rack. This meant enduring an eight-hour shift washing trucks and buses out in a large enclosed bay area with high-powered hoses and industrial strength soap. Even worse, it also translated to a full day of wearing drenched clothing. It was useless to complain. I'd heard more times than I could count, "The needs of the military come first."

There was no concrete way for me to complain of Rustin's treatment without sounding like a whiner.

So, instead of complaining, I would find ways to turn the wash rack into a fun rack. I invented competitions among the airmen, like racing to see which team could wash and wax a bus the fastest, which airmen could make it through the day with the driest clothes, etc. We listened to music, laughed, shared stories, and "accidentally" hosed one another to make our days enjoyable.

I soon found my niche. I actually began to amuse the guys by creating silly games and playing pranks to keep some balance between work and on-the- job socializing. I'd created a midnight shift game that required every officer working the street to incorporate a "word" into their radio traffic before the end of shift. Afterward we would vote to see who had the most daring or unique word usage, and I would ceremoniously hand them a prize. Would you believe, I bought toy trinkets from the dollar store as prize giveaways? The guys actually looked forward to receiving their cap guns, finger puppets, racecars and whoopee cushions.

The game went like this; I'd tell them they'd have to say "camel" over the air and somehow incorporate it into their call without being found out by a supervisor. One officer called in to say that he would be speaking with a group of juveniles in a park who appeared to be smoking Camels. Another time, the word was "hairball." The winning officer said to the dispatcher, "Could you please secure the sally port" (prisoner garage door), then he cleared his throat and continued: "Excuse me dispatch, I had hairball in my throat."

Another fun game I created to pass dead street time between the hours of 3:30 and 6 a.m. was the most obscure ticket contest. The officers would consult their ordinance violations and write warning tickets to the residents for infractions such as failure to post house numbers or overgrown weeds. In hindsight, I'm sure the shift supervisor scratched his head on those days. Tickets like those probably hadn't been given since the ordinances were created.

Once I started a game that entailed creating the most unusual officer initiated calls for service. One winning officer called into the dispatcher and said, "I'll be out of my car momentarily to re-erect a 'For Sale' sign that fell over in a front yard." I called in one, "dispatch, could you please log a dead black cat in the roadway at 35th and Armitage." The dispatchers always responded quizzically and with slight hesitation, "ten-four?" Not until we would go out drinking socially at a lounge, which opened specifically for the police at 7 a.m., would we clue in the perplexed dispatchers.

It seemed that one guy, Officer Flynn, would win most of the shift games. Knowing he was willing to go the extra mile on nearly everything, I took an opportunity to test his manhood. After roll call, I ceremoniously presented Flynn with a prize for the previous night's shenanigans. I came across one of those Mexican vehicle-ceiling skirts made of velvet with religious emblems and little dingle berry balls hanging from the bottom. The guys roared with laughter as Flynn unwrapped this unusual gift. I then announced, "Now, this isn't just a prize, Flynn has to attach it to the interior ceiling of his squad and drive to every officer's beat to prove he affixed it properly.

This was extremely daring when you considered that officers could not leave their beat without permission from the shift supervisor. If Flynn received a call for service, he risked the citizens seeing the ceiling skirt. He also risked having the supervisor show up and see it. So Flynn's primary goal was to race from beat to beat and receive acknowledgement from at least ten different police units without being caught. Needless to say, Flynn succeeded. Days after, without another thought to the incident, a police lieutenant performed a surprise inspection. Flynn later showed me his evaluation...Cleanliness: acceptable, but please remove religious items from the trunk.

Can you see a pattern here? There are numerous ways you can make any work condition fun if you allow yourself to be creative.

Client Story

Last year I had a client, Jimmy, who loathed his job. He put so much time and energy into focusing on what was so awful about his job he literally put himself into his own prison. Do you know people like this? Are you one of them? Here's how Jimmy's story played out.

Jimmy: I feel stuck. I'm the sole provider for my wife and two daughters because I never wanted my wife to work. I wanted to have a family with a stay-at-home Mom because that's what my Mom did and I loved having her around. I worked for the Post Office for eight years, had great benefits, and made a little extra money on the side helping with home renovations. I lost my job at the Post Office two years ago and lost my family medical benefits. I scrambled to find work and took the first thing I was offered which is where I still am now, at the moving company. The homeowners treat us like slaves and expect us to be incompetent.

Me: That has to be very frustrating.

Jimmy: It is. I'm better than that. Sometimes I just want to break something on purpose to piss them off.

Me: I get it. Sometimes we need an outlet to let go of our anger.

After our initial discussion about ways that Jimmy could let out his frustration and/or reframe the situation when someone got under his skin, I asked him some specific questions about his experiences.

Me: Help me understand something, Jimmy. Were you happy working at the Post Office?

Jimmy: It was a good job. I didn't love it, but it had good benefits.

Me: You also mentioned you used to do renovation work on the side. Did you enjoy that?

Jimmy: I love using my hands to build things. I feel like I am responsible for creating something that people can appreciate.

Me: What prevented you from doing renovation work full-time?

Jimmy: Ten years ago, before I met my wife, my uncle told me that the Post Office was hiring, so I applied and got it. I always loved renovation work and did cash jobs since I was sixteen but didn't want to have to go through the apprentice program with the Union. I think I was just a dumb, naive kid looking to make an easy buck.

Me: So if I understand correctly, you love renovation work, have been doing it for more than sixteen years, but have not explored how you can make a lucrative living doing it today?

Jimmy: I suppose. But it's not so easy to start that now. I'm Thirty-two years old and have mouths to feed.

Me: Thirty-two is far from old. The good news is that, unlike most people I work with, you already know what you love to do. That's the biggest obstacle. I would like you to describe a perfect day at work.

Jimmy: Right now?

Me: Right now!

Jimmy: I'm an early bird so I'd wake-up at 5:00 AM and be at work by 6:00 AM. I would be in the Carpenters' Union because I love building things, and they have great benefits. I'd have the best tool kit so I could deliver quality work. People would compliment my work and I would go home everyday feeling like "the man."

Me: Awesome Jimmy. You have a great vision.

Jimmy: Yeah, but most carpenter's apprentices start when they're in their early twenties.

As you can see, Jimmy was holding on to a belief that he was too old to do what he loved. I've worked with many clients who have held similar beliefs that prevented them from reinventing themselves. Everything from gender, age, physicality, sexual orientation to, "I'm not smart enough" or "I'm an introvert".

Me: Do you think anyone over thirty has ever joined the Carpenters' Union?

Jimmy: Maybe. I'm not sure.

Me: Do you think you'd have an advantage over the younger guys because you've been doing renovations for sixteen years already?

Jimmy: Oh, I'd smoke 'em! (Laughs)

Me: Of course, you would! (Laughing)

Jimmy: I just don't know how I'd be able to go to school for the program and still feed my family.

I'm very careful not to give my clients all of the solutions in my coaching. I've found that people become more empowered and attached to their outcomes and goals when they have to dig deep within themselves for the answers.

Me: How do you suppose you can go to apprentice school five days a week for the first twelve weeks and still handle providing for your family?

Jimmy: I could probably do renovation work a few nights a week and on the weekends. It's just a matter of getting my name out there to people.

Me: How would you do that?

Jimmy: I can call all my past clients and get referrals.

Me: What else?

Jimmy: I can post on Craig's list.

Me: Great. What else?

Jimmy: Umm, I'm not sure. (Pauses) Oh, I could advertise it on Facebook.

Me: Awesome!

Jimmy: This is great. I feel like my heart's gonna beat out of my chest!

Me: Why?

Jimmy: Because I always knew I wanted to do renovations and building and I kept making excuses about why I wasn't doing it. Now I feel relieved.

Me: Jimmy, I'm really excited for you.

When people are attached to doing what they love, they will usually start to take action immediately. However, people can also fall off or get distracted every so often because of old habits and patterns. The final process with Jimmy was building an action plan that held him accountable to his short-term goals and supported him during some of the obstacles that would inevitably arise as he began to take steps forward.

Jimmy is now a full-time carpenter in the union and comes home from work every day feeling like "the man."

> *Don't ask yourself what the world needs; ask yourself what makes you come alive. And then go and do that. Because what the world needs are people who have come alive.*
>
> **—Harold Whitman**

IN YOUR QUEST TO DISCOVER YOUR TRUE CALLING, ENTERTAIN THESE QUESTIONS FOR A MOMENT:

What if you believed you were put here to solve a problem? Would that knowledge compel you to open up your options? What would they be?

All successful people and companies solve problems for people. Whether or not you endorse the following brands is irrelevant; this exercise is simply a means to show you how brands became massively successful and iconic worldwide because they solved a problem in the world market. Look at the following brands to get a better idea of how they delivered on their mission statements:

Gucci: the price is forgotten long after the quality remains.

Mercedes-Benz: The six values that "drive" Mercedes-Benz USA are:

- The audacity to reject compromise
- The instinct to protect what matters
- The commitment to honor a legacy
- The vision to consider every detail
- The foresight to take responsibility
- The ingenuity to outperform expectations

"We give of our best for customers who expect the best, and we live a culture of excellence that is based on shared values."

Louis Vuitton: The LVMH mission statement says, "The mission of the LVMH group is to represent the most refined qualities of Western 'Art de Vivre' around the world. LVMH must continue to be synonymous with both elegance and creativity. Our products and the cultural values they embody blend tradition and innovation, and kindle dream and fantasy."

Disney: Disney's Mission Statement states, "The mission of The Walt Disney Company is to be one of the world's leading producers and providers of entertainment and information."

Amazon: Amazon's vision is to be Earth's most customer centric company; to build a place where people can come to find and discover anything they might want to buy online.

Apple: Apple is committed to bringing the best personal computing experience to students, educators, creative professionals and consumers around the world through its innovative hardware, software and Internet products. Apple is committed to creating fun, functional products that perform flawlessly for consumers.

Facebook: Facebook's mission is to give people the power to share and make the world more open and connected.

Google: Google's mission is to organize the world's information and make it universally accessible and useful.

Skype: Skype's mission is to be the fabric of real-time communication on the web.

YouTube: YouTube's mission is to provide fast and easy video access and the ability to share videos frequently

Coca-Cola: Coke solves the problem for the world's desire for a sweet carbonated beverage to quench their thirst.

Nike: Solves the problem of the world's desire for quality athletic wear by offering to "bring inspiration and innovation to every athlete in the world".

Virgin: Solves the problem of the world's desire to make a difference by offering solutions to the world's major issues.

Starbucks: Solves the problem of satiating the world's coffee desire by inspiring and nurturing the human spirit—one person, one cup, and one neighborhood at a time.

McDonald's: Solves the problem of satiating hunger with quick inexpensive eats to "be our customer's favorite place and way to eat".

Lisa Lockwood, the Reinvention Expert's mission: I am dedicated to bringing people back to joy by reattaching them to their dream career.

I hope that after learning about these brands and their missions you can begin to have a better idea of where you fit in the world. Sadly, some people never discover what problem they were meant to solve, and thus languish in a life of mediocrity. They take what life offers which, in essence, are the leftovers. I know you're not one of them because you are reading this book.

I am certain when you find your passion the following will happen:

- You will have endless energy.
- Time will disappear.
- You will be extremely happy.

The million-dollar questions I'm often asked are "how do I discover what I'm meant to do and what problems do I solve?"

The answer is not always cut and dry, but there are many clues that can assist you with this answer. Consider these:

- What we love the most, what we speak about, think about, and dream about are significant clues as to our mission.
- What we fear and what we're excited about equally are clues as to what we should be doing.

Trust that your mission will enable others to succeed.

Narrow down what you enjoy, love, and value in your life. Spend a few minutes reflecting on these questions and writing down the first thoughts that come to mind without editing.

What are the five traits you liked in yourself as a child?

_____
_____
_____
_____
_____

What do I want my life to be like?

_____
_____
_____
_____

What do I want to give?

_____
_____
_____
_____

What would my ideal environment be?

_____
_____
_____

What do I want to do with my time?

_____

_____

_____

When was I most happy?

_____

_____

_____

What made me happy?

_____

_____

_____

What are my strengths?

_____

_____

_____

What are my talents and gifts?

_____

_____

_____

What are all of the assets I bring to the table?

_____

_____

_____

How do I most enjoy contributing to others?

_____

_____

_____

What cause do I most want to serve?

_____

_____

_____

EXERCISE

Recall ways you have solved problems for other people. Compile a long list of ways you've helped people in your life until you start to get some clarity on your purpose.

_____
_____
_____
_____
_____
_____
_____
_____
_____
_____
_____
_____
_____
_____
_____
_____
_____
_____
_____
_____

Your Name: _____

Solves the problem: _____

> **ANOTHER GREAT WAY TO DISCOVER YOUR MISSION IS TO ASK YOUR FRIENDS THE FOLLOWING TEN QUESTIONS. SEND THESE QUESTIONS TO FOUR PEOPLE:**
>
> 1. Describe something that I consistently do well.
> 2. Name one thing you've seen me do well.
> 3. Tell me the best thing about how I look.
> 4. In as much detail as possible, describe a time when I seemed to be the happiest.
> 5. Tell me what you think my strongest traits are.
> 6. If you were going to describe my best strengths, what three words would you use?
> 7. Describe a situation where you think I might be of service.
> 8. Tell me what you respect about me.
> 9. Describe me as an animal. What kind would I be and why?
> 10. Describe me as a car. What kind would I be and why?

Let's not confuse life missions with careers you may have had or jobs you may have held for many years to make ends meet or earn a living. We often fall into careers and jobs out of necessity, to please others or because we think it's something we should be doing.

EXERCISE

Start a journal. Create a written description of your future in the most creative possible way. Envision scenes from your future. Do not censor yourself. Fill an entire notebook. Let it flow. Any flash or vision that shows up, write it down. Do this for twenty to thirty minutes a day. Keep doing this. Only you will know when the process is over. Trust then that you will have discovered your mission!

Patience, persistence and perspiration make an unbeatable combination for success.

—Napoleon Hill

• *Chapter Five* •

PERSEVERANCE

#5 Passion, Obsession, Persistence

There is a difference between interest and commitment. When you're interested in doing something, you do it only when it is convenient. When you're committed to doing something, you accept no excuses, only results.

Would you agree that your obsession determines your habits? Achievers do daily what losers do occasionally. Where do you fit into this equation? We all have setbacks. Even achievers are occasionally derailed, but the difference between the achievers and the people living in mediocre land is that the achievers get back on track a hell of a lot faster.

Perseverance is the hard work you do after you get
tired of doing the hard work you already did.
—Newt Gingrich

Inspiring Examples of Passion, Obsession and Persistence

- If Howard Schultz gave up after being turned down by banks 242 times, there would be no Starbucks.
- If J.K. Rowling stopped after being turned down by multiple publishers for years, there would be no Harry Potter.
- If Walt Disney quit too soon after his theme park concept was trashed 302 times, there would be no Disneyland.
- If this singer gave up in 1954 when Jimmy Denny, manager of the Grand Ole Opry fired him after one performance telling him, "You

ain't goin' nowhere, son. You ought to go back to drivin' a truck," there would be no Elvis.

- If Jack Canfield stopped after being rejected by over 140 publishers, there would be no *Chicken Soup for the Soul*. This title went on to sell over eight million copies in forty-one languages.
- If Colonel Sanders at seventy-five years old stopped after soliciting over 1,000 places to sell his chicken recipe of eleven herbs and spices, we wouldn't have Kentucky Fried Chicken, which later sold for a finger-licken' $15 million!

MAKE THESE POWERFUL STATEMENTS A PART OF YOUR DAILY MANTRA:

I will fight for it.

I will NOT give up.

I will reach my goal.

Absolutely nothing will stop me.

One thing is for sure, if you give up too soon, you'll never know what you'll be missing. Keep going and NEVER quit. Every minute of your life is an opportunity to advance in your reinvention. Speak about your mission at any and every engagement you are called upon to attend. Absorb as much information on your mission and field of expertise, and become consumed by it!

Now I'd like to share a few biographies from the lives of respected successful political world figures who will serve as an example of the title of this chapter—*Passion-Obsession-Persistence*. Pay close attention to the timeline of obstacles listed after each brief biography and ask yourself if you'd be able to persist at this level.

Martin Luther King, Jr.

Martin Luther King, Jr. graduated high school at the age of fifteen and went on to earn a fellowship from Crozer Theological Seminary along with his Doctorate from Boston University. In 1955, as a member of the executive committee of the National Association for the Advancement of Colored People, he led the first great Negro nonviolent demonstration of contemporary times in the United States, the bus boycott that lasted 382 days. On December 21, 1956, after the Supreme Court had declared unconstitutional the laws requiring segregation on buses, Negroes and whites rode the buses as equals. Although he was arrested, abused, and his home bombed, he emerged as a true leader in the civil rights movement. Over the next eleven years as President of the Southern Christian Leadership Conference, King traveled over six million miles and spoke over twenty-five hundred times and wrote five books and numerous articles. At the age of thirty-five, he was the youngest man to receive the Nobel Peace Prize.

1951   oins the bus boycott after Rosa Parks was arrested on December 1st.

1956   His home was bombed.

1958   Is nearly killed when stabbed by an assailant in Harlem while on a speaking tour.

1960   Arrested in Atlanta during a sit-in waiting to be served at a restaurant. He is sentenced to four months in jail but released after intervention by John and Robert Kennedy.

1962   During the unsuccessful Albany, GA movement, King is arrested on July 27th and jailed.

1963   On Good Friday, April 12th, he is arrested along with Ralph Abernathy by police commissioner Eugene "Bull" Connor for demonstrating without a permit.

1964   During the summer, King experiences his first hurtful rejection by black people when he is stoned by black Muslims in Harlem.

1965   On February 2nd, he is arrested in Selma, AL during a voting rights demonstration.

1966   On January 22nd, King moves into a Chicago slum tenement to attract attention to the living conditions of the poor.

1967   The Supreme Court upholds the conviction of MLK by a Birmingham, AL court for demonstrating without a permit. King spends four days in a Birmingham jail.

1968   On March 28th, he leads a march that turns violent. This was the first time one of his events led to violence. At sunset on April 4th, Martin Luther King is fatally shot while standing on the balcony of the Lorraine Motel in Memphis, TN.

Mohandas Gandhi

In 1893, Gandhi went to South Africa, where he spent 20 years opposing discriminatory legislation against Indians. As a pioneer of Satyagraha, or resistance through mass non-violent civil disobedience, he became one of the major political and spiritual leaders of his time. Satyagraha remains one of the most potent philosophies in freedom struggles throughout the world today.

In 1914, Gandhi returned to India, where he supported the Home Rule movement, and became leader of the Indian National Congress, advocating a policy of non-violent non-co-operation to achieve independence. His goal was to help poor farmers and laborers protest oppressive taxation and discrimination. He struggled to alleviate poverty, liberate women and put an end to caste discrimination, with the ultimate objective being self-rule for India.

Even after his death, Gandhi's commitment to non-violence and his belief in simple living—making his own clothes, eating a vegetarian diet, and using fasts for self-purification as well as a means of protest—have been a beacon of hope for oppressed and marginalized people throughout the world.

1891   Fails as a lawyer in India.

1893   Accepts commission to spend a year in South Africa advising on a lawsuit.

1899   Outbreak of Boer War (1899-1901) in South Africa. Gandhi organizes an ambulance corps for the British.

1901   Returns to India to attend the Indian National Congress. G.K. Gokhale introduces him to nationalist leaders.

1901-1906

    Struggles toward Brahmacharya (celibacy), finally ending his sexual activity in 1906.

1907   The Boer Republic Transvaal, now under the control of the British, attempts to register all Indians as members; Gandhi and others refuse to register. Their resistance efforts mark the first use of nonviolent non-cooperation by the Indian minority in South Africa, soon called satyagraha, or "soul-force."

1908   Arrested and sentenced to two months in prison. Later that year in October, Gandhi is arrested again, spends another month in jail.

1914   Arrives in England, just at the outbreak of World War I.

1919   Nationalists hold a hartal, or day of fasting and prayer, in protest of the Rowlatt Act, which drastically curtails civil liberties in India. On April 13, 1919, under General Dyer, British troops slaughter Indian protestors during the Amritsar Massacre.

1920   Calls for a period of non-cooperation across India.

1922   Arrested for sedition.

March 1922-January 1924

Gandhi remains in prison.

1924-1928

Avoids politics, focusing his writings on the improvement of India.

1925   Despite his long absence from politics, Gandhi becomes President of the Indian National Congress.

1930   Publishes the Declaration of Independence of India.

1931   Arrested for violating the Salt Laws; non-cooperation movements break out across India.

1932   Arrested for sedition, and held without a trial. Gandhi fasts in prison to protest the treatment of untouchables.

1939   World War II begins, lasting until 1945.

1942   Sir Stafford Cripps arrives in India, presenting to the Indian National Congress a proposal for Dominion status (autonomy within the British Commonwealth) after the War. The Indian National Congress rejects the Cripps proposal and declares it will grant its support for the British war effort only in return for independence.

August 1942
>   Congressional leaders are arrested; Gandhi is imprisoned in
>   the Aga Khan's palace.

February 10 to March 2, 1943
>   Gandhi fasts while imprisoned, to protest British rule.

January 30, 1948
>   Gandhi is assassinated by Nathuram Vinayuk Godse, a Hindu
>   nationalist.

August-December 1948
>   India dissolves into chaos and killings, as Hindus and
>   Muslims flee for the borders of India and Pakistan.

Abraham Lincoln

Abraham Lincoln is regarded by many historians and laymen as the foremost of our Presidents and greatest American of all time. He is viewed as the savior of the American union and the "Great Emancipator." Throughout his life, Abraham Lincoln overcame one obstacle after another, from having a minimal education and challenges in his personal life, to his career as a lawyer, politician and leader of our country. Through it all, he always supported what he believed in and, despite being knocked down and defeated again and again, managed to reinvent himself each time. He is another amazing inspiration and model of what's possible when you believe in your vision. Following is a list of Abraham Lincoln's challenges and accomplishments:

1832   Lost his job, defeated in his bid for legislature.

1833   Failed in business.

1834   Elected to legislature.

1835   sweetheart Ann Rutledge dies.

1836   Lincoln has a nervous breakdown.

1838   Defeated for Speaker of House position.

1843   Defeated for nomination to Congress.

1846   Elected to Congress.

1848   Lost renomination to Congress.

1849   Rejected for position of Land Officer.

1854   Defeated in his bid for Senate.

1856   Defeated for nomination as Vice President.

1858   Defeated again for Senate.
1860   Elected President of United States.

I am not what happens to me. I am what I choose to become.

—Carl Jung

EXERCISE

Write down six goals for the week—three goals in the material world (e.g. exercising, writing an article, learning something new in marketing) and three goals in the spiritual world (e.g. taking a walk in nature, meditating, practicing yoga).

Material world goals

1. _____
2. _____
3. _____

Spiritual world goals

1. _____
2. _____
3. _____

In your new journal, create a written log of how you spend your time for one week, being completely honest. This will let you see, with dazzling clarity, exactly how much time you use productively and how much you waste. Notice the patterns. Carry over goals not attained. Write down the reasons you didn't achieve your weekly goals. Identify the obvious time wasters. How will you get rid of them? Give yourself a date when these time wasters will be gone forever!

Hell begins on the day when God grants us a clear vision of all that we might have achieved, of all the gifts we wasted, of all that we might have done that we did not do.

—Giancarlo Menotti

• *Chapter Six* •

CLEAR VISION

#6 Create a Vision Board

People are usually better at distinguishing what they don't want in their lives than they are at figuring out what they do want. I was one of those people. Having attended a plethora of seminars and workshops geared toward getting clarity on what I truly wanted to do with my life, I can tell you that hashing out what I didn't want opened the door to understanding more of what I did desire in my life.

Remember when I said that we reinvent ourselves based on either the cause or effect of our immediate situation? Most people, initially, reinvent out of necessity.

The secret to success is to begin to reinvent because of our clear vision of our dreams and our passion to live them. There are plenty of examples of well-known people who have an undeniable gift and passion toward a life-long sustainable career. If you embody any extraordinary gifts and you've shelved them, take a look at these examples to serve as an inspiration for what is possible if you were to re-ignite them.

Wayne Gretzky

When Wayne Gretzky was six years old, he would skate for hours right in his own backyard in the rink built by his father, Walter Gretzky. It was here that he mastered his shooting, skating, and stick handling skills, learning everything about the game of hockey from his dad. With each passing season of peewee hockey, his skills increased dramatically, setting multiple scoring records including a mind-boggling 378-goal season in his last year playing peewee hockey. Along the way, he earned the nickname "White Tornado" because of his speed and skill, and the fact that he wore white hockey gloves.

Throughout his teenage years in Canada, Gretzky continued to set records and lead the teams he played for until finally he wound up in the NHL, joining the Edmonton Oilers in 1979. It was during his first season in the NHL that he won the Hart trophy, the first time a first-year player was awarded this honor.

Starting with the 1980-81 season, Gretzky began an all-out assault on scoring records, winning his first of seven straight scoring titles. Along the way, he did what no other player in the history of the NHL has ever done, scoring more than 200 points in a single season. Gretzky did this four times during his landmark career! He also played in the All-Star game every season he was in the NHL along with claiming the all-time goal scoring and overall point scoring titles along with many other honors. After his retirement, he was inducted into the Hall of Fame and consistently is rated the greatest hockey player of all time by fans, players and veterans in the world of hockey.

Warren Buffet

Before Warren Buffet finished elementary school, he had an interest in making money and building wealth. His services ranged from selling magazines, Coca-Cola, and chewing gum door-to-door, to working in his Grandfather's grocery store. His moneymaking pursuits carried over into high school where he delivered newspapers, sold various products from golf balls to postage stamps, detailed cars and began his first venture into coin-operated vending with the purchase of several used pinball machines. He purchased his first shares of stock when he was eleven and from there his entrepreneurial spirit thrived throughout his young adult life.

During his college years, Buffet focused his attention on business, graduating from the University of Nebraska with a BS in Business Administration and then earning his MS in Economics from Columbia Business School. As a result of his various investments along the way, including investing in a company owned by his father along with a farm that included a tenant farmer to work the land, Warren Buffet left college with savings close to $100,000 (measured in 2010 dollars).

When someone is so focused and passionate about something, successes just keep adding up. Warren Buffet's bank account is a reflection of his focus and passion for money. In 2008, Forbes magazine ranked him the richest man in the world with an estimated worth of sixty-two billion dollars, give or take a billion depending on the year. He continues to be one of my all-time favorite financial inspirations.

Barbra Streisand

Barbra Joan Streisand is one of the most successful entertainers in modern entertainment history. Her work as a singer, actress, writer, director and film producer have earned her two Academy Awards, eight Grammys, five Emmys, a special Tony Award along with numerous others, making her one of a handful of entertainers who have won all four of the major awards in the entertainment industry.

According to the Recording Industry Association of America, Streisand holds the record for the most top-ten albums of any female recording artist, a total of thirty-one since the early days of her career in 1963. In true reinvention style, Barbara Streisand continues to reinvent herself and stay current with the music industry. After almost fifty years, she produced her latest top-ten album, creating the widest span (forty-eight years) between first and latest top-ten albums of any female recording artist. She is also one of the rare artists to achieve number-one albums in five consecutive decades.

Whether you're a fan of her brand of entertainment or not, you must respect her for continually evolving and following her passion for music, acting and sharing her gifts as an entertainer throughout her life. She's truly an inspiration and seems to know a thing or two about reinvention as well.

Justin Bieber

As a child, Justin Bieber showed a strong interest in music and taught himself to play several instruments. His accelerated rise to stardom is largely due to his mother posting numerous performances on YouTube. A true overnight success, he followed his heart all along the way and landed in the big time complete with a record deal and debut album, *My World*, all within two years. He reminds me that combining passion with focus and energy can propel you to great heights in a very short amount of time.

Akiane

Akiane Kramarik is another example of passion meets talent meets drive and determination. She began expressing herself as an artist at the age of four and continues to develop her passion for art through her paintings, drawings and poetry. I am continually amazed at her level of dedication and commitment to her work. She spends anywhere between one to two hundred hours on each painting, routinely getting up at 4:00 AM to begin work in her studio.

Some people are taken down a certain path and influenced, through environment and conditioning, to follow a particular course. Essentially, they were pushed to excel in their fields—a form of reinvention by effect versus reinvention by choice.

Andre Agassi

In his autobiography, Agassi writes, "I play tennis for a living even though I hate tennis, hate it with a dark and secret passion and always have." As a child, his father demanded that he play, creating a regimented environment that included a machine called "the dragon" that would shoot tennis balls at the young Agassi at 100 miles per hour. Agassi would later refer to this experience as his "backyard prison".

Michael Jackson

Michael Jackson had a troubled childhood, in particular with his father, Joseph. Michael claimed to be the victim of physical, emotional and verbal abuse on a regular basis from his father who was a strict disciplinarian. Michael first spoke openly about his childhood abuse during an interview with Oprah Winfrey in 1993. Ten years later during an interview with Martin Bashir, Jackson acknowledged that his father hurt him when he was a child, but also said his father's strict discipline played a huge role in his success.

Venus and Serena Williams

Venus and Serena Williams trail into professional tennis was blazed by their father, Richard, who loved the game of tennis. For six hours a day they would practice with old equipment on worn-out tennis courts as their Dad coached and instructed them from information he read from tennis instruction manuals. The pair began competing before they were five years old, and as a result, both have earned the rank of World Number One at least three times throughout their careers.

Client Story

Several years ago, a client of mine, Kristen, was struggling in her relationships and was extremely dissatisfied in her career as an attorney. Kristen was a brilliant woman. She had always excelled academically and recently made partner in a prestigious, world-renowned law-firm. It was a rigorous climb. She was on call around the clock. She endured the pressures of delivering for the firm and her clients to the detriment of her social life. What you must know about Kristen is that her father had set Kristen on the path of becoming a lawyer from the tender age of twelve. Everyone who knew Kristen was made aware that she would be a lawyer. This may not seem surprising to many of the people reading this today. There are numerous cultures in a society where the career path is decided by one's parents. The children are groomed to follow a particular path without consent. Most of the time they are so sold on that path that they've forgotten that it was not their idea to begin with.

As Kristen achieved her desire to reach partner in the law firm, she realized that she was extremely unhappy. Often, in cases like this, people look for ways to circumvent their sadness by indulging in a myriad of means in which to seek pleasure. I've coached clients who became addicts via food, sex, shopping, or drugs. Kristen used shopping to mask the pain of her grueling career. In addition to an unfulfilling career, Kristen was striking out on her quest to find a mate.

When someone is sad or angry on a daily basis because of their work, that energy is inevitably brought into all areas of their life. I listened as Kristen explained that she had a pattern of attracting men who were emotionally unavailable or men who cheated on her. It was so bad that she would tell her friends that she should be a lesbian or that men were merely accessories.

Can you see how thoughts such as theses perpetuated the exact thing that Kristen declared? As our time together progressed, I learned that once Kristen achieved her law firm partnership she became even more stressed.

> **Me**: What kind of work do you find satisfying?
> **Kristen**: I love to teach.
> **Me**: What's preventing you from teaching now?
> **Kristen**: There's no money in teaching. I'd be making a quarter of what I'm making now.

Me: Are you in debt?

Kristen: I just completed paying off my student loans! I have a condo, a car payment and a second home that I just began renovating.

Me: How much time do you spend enjoying your car, condo, and second home?

Kristen: Nowhere near as much as I'd like to enjoy them. I know where you're going, Lisa. It's not that easy. How do I just throw away all of that education? I worked my ass off to be where I am!

Me: And I can see how happy all of that work made you.

Kristen: Touché.

Me: Kristen, I'm your ally. I'm not trying to be a ball-buster, but I am not going to sugarcoat any of this for you.

Kristen: So what are you saying? You want me to up and quit the law firm and apply for a teaching job?

Me: I'm not saying that at all. I am attempting to reconnect you to what you love. You told me that you love teaching. What I'd like you to do is look at the reasons you're providing for what is preventing you from doing what you love every day.

Kristen: Can we switch topics?

When I've hit a nerve with a client, it's normal for them to want to bail. My goal is to ask the poignant questions that will deliver a sting. However, I also know that if I push too hard, they won't come back for round two, so I honored Kristen's request to change the topic.

Me: Sure.

Kristen: Are you telling me that it's my fault that I'm attracting all of these cheats and heartbreakers?

Me: How available are you for a full-on nurturing relationship?

Kristen: Listen, I'm not one of those women who depend on a man. I believe in pre-nups, and I believe a woman needs to be fiercely independent. Men are not a meal ticket!

It was obvious that Kristen's response was coming from a place of pain. She had been let down by the men in her life for many years and had put them into a category of distastefulness.

Me: Why do you want to be in a relationship?

Kristen: I want to share my life experiences with someone.

Me: Let's pretend you're in a relationship right now. What are some of the things you'd be sharing with Mr. Man?

Kristen: (Giggles) Not much, he'd be hearing quite a bit about how miserable I am at work. I'd be canceling dates with him regularly because my career comes first. Geeeeeez, I wouldn't even date me!

Me: (I laugh) Kristen I know you're a strong independent woman and you should be very proud of that. And can you see how the men you have dated in the past, never felt as if they held a special place in your life?

Because Kristen made it clear that the men she dated weren't very significant, they chose not to stick around.

Kristen: So now what?

Me: Tell me how a man can make you feel special (significant).

Often, the very emotions we want to experience are the same emotions our significant other wants to feel and experience. I ended our session together by giving Kristen time to do some homework. She was assigned to create a Vision Board of the kind of man she wanted to attract. I also recommended a book called *The Five Love Languages* by Gary Chapman This book helps people understand how they feel loved and how their partner feels loved.

Kristen: I can't believe how much clarity I have now. I wrote down all of the characteristics I wanted in a partner, and I felt a sense of relief. Aside from him loving rock music, hockey and travel, I want him to be intelligent and have a creative outlet.

Nowhere in Kristen's description of an ideal mate did she include his income level or physical characteristics. When I brought that to her attention she laughed and said, "I didn't even think about that."

I found this to be a beautiful quality in Kristen because I believed she really did the exercise from her heart.

Me: I'm extremely proud of you, Kristen. You permitted yourself to become vulnerable and authentic. Do you still believe all men are cheats?

Kristen: You're not setting me up with that question. (Laughs) I realize women cheat too, and it doesn't benefit me to stereotype.

After four months, Kristen decided to leave her law-firm and was hired full-time to teach at a prestigious University. As she was transitioning into her teaching career, she fell in love and married a successful man who loves rock music, hockey, and travel and shares her love of literature, poetry and history. If Kristen had not put in the effort to create a vision of what she wanted in her life, there's a very good chance she would have continued on her former path.

My Story

After *Undercover Angel* was published, I officially reinvented myself into an author. I remember the day my advance copy arrived in the mail, and the dream and vision became something tangible. I had birthed a new beginning. That beginning opened the door to even more reinventions. I was put into in a place where I needed to learn everything about marketing, media interviews, and setting up book signings and events. Because I self-published, I was truly on my own with this venture. I began to create my vision for what I wanted for *Undercover Angel*. It looked like this:

1. National Media Tour
2. National Television Interviews
3. Local TV USA & Canada
4. Radio Interviews
5. Newspaper Articles
6. Magazine Interviews
7. Get my book into Barnes & Noble and Borders (which was still in business in 2007)
8. Do book signings
9. Get my book into specialty stores
10. Speaking Engagements
11. More Coaching Clients

12. Book Sales
13. Hire an Assistant
14. Sign with an Agent
15. Hire a Publicist
16. Find a Screenwriter

Once the checklist was created, I began to take action. I was so excited and connected to the vision of having the contents of my story serve as a means to educate, inspire, and entertain others that time just disappeared. Can you relate to the feeling of being so on purpose with your mission that sleeping and eating become an inconvenience? That was exactly how I felt. My husband nicknamed me "Grindstone" because I would grind out work until the last possible moment. If anyone at home was looking for me, they would find me in my home office.

Another amazing thing about being in alignment with your mission is that synchronistic events and circumstances start to happen. I'll share a few of mine with you.

1. When Undercover Angel was featured in The Chicago Tribune, I received an email from a woman I had met years ago. She wasn't more than an acquaintance, but wanted to congratulate me on my book. After a few emails and a phone call, I discovered that she too was a writer and an editor. She had some experience in book marketing, and I soon realized that I had found my new assistant!

2. I was listening to an interview by *Rich Dad, Poor Dad* author Robert Kyosaki, and he was sharing the story of how he self-published and had a garage full of books he wasn't able to get bookstores to carry. He came up with an idea to circumvent the bookstore system of not carrying self-published books. He would phone the bookstore and tell the store manager that he was on a book tour and would be doing many local TV and radio shows, and he would like their bookstore to host his book signing. Once the bookstore heard the author would be bringing attention to their store through TV and radio they said yes! When Kyosaki contacted all of the local radio stations and television stations to tell them that he would be on a book tour, doing a signing at such and such bookstore, they wanted

to be involved and cover the story. His book was originally self-published before being picked up commercially to become a *New York Times* bestseller. To date, the book has sold twenty-six million copies and has become a household name. He focused on talk shows and radio show appearances, which had the biggest influence on book sales at the time. Guess who used the same template for her very first book signing in Las Vegas? I did, and it worked. Now, I now had "social proof" as an author and was deemed newsworthy, inspiring other TV networks to follow suit and book me.

3. I knew it was important to have a press release. I didn't have experience writing one, so I leveraged that out to the professionals, and my assistant, to create an online presence for my book tour. PRWeb was contracted in 2007 to launch my book tour. Several months later, with only one local news TV interview under my belt, I was contacted by the producers of *The Big Idea with Donnie Deutsch* to appear on the show. I landed my first National TV interview as a self-published author!

4. One afternoon, my publicist contacted me and asked if I was sitting down. One of the *Oprah* producers had contacted her to find out if I'd be interested in a story they were running about strong women. Interested? *Oprah* was going on summer hiatus and, eventually, they decided to scrap the story, but it left me on a magical high for several months.

5. While doing an interview for a radio show geared toward police officers, the host told me that I should get in contact with one of his friends regarding getting *Undercover Angel* a book-to-movie deal. Turns out that friend was Joe Pistone, also known as Donny Brasco! Donny Brasco later gave *Undercover Angel* a beautiful testimonial, set me up with an agent, and is still my dear friend.

My Life Vision on a Board

A vision board is typically a poster board used to display a collage of images. When you surround yourself with images of what you want to become, what you want to have, where you want to live, or where you want to vacation, your life changes to match those images and those desires. Your mission must become your obsession for you to do incredible things with it. Use a physical or virtual dream-board of photos, virtual images, and powerful quotes for additional incentives and reinforcements. They even have virtual vision boards now using popular websites and tools like Pinterest. Look me up if you visit.

Before you begin your vision board, no matter what method you are using, I recommend getting centered. You have to create your vision in your mind. Look for a place where you can sit quietly and ponder what you want in life. Set your intention for your vision board. With lots of kindness and openness, ask yourself what you want. Maybe images will come into your head. Just take a moment to be with them. This process makes building your vision board a deeper experience. It gives a chance for your ego to step aside so you can create your vision with ease.

> *Music washes away from the soul the dust of everyday life.*
>
> **—Berthold Auerbach**

STIMULATE YOUR INTUITIVE AND EMOTIONAL SENSES NOT JUST YOUR PRIMARY FIVE SENSES (SIGHT, SOUND, TASTE, TOUCH, SMELL):

- Sense of destiny
- Sense of what's possible
- Sense of awe
- Sense of humility
- Sense of generosity
- Sense of knowing
- Sense of passion
- Sense of belonging

Put on soft music. Use the same music you would use for getting a massage or any activity where you want to keep your mind quiet. If you are indoors, consider lighting a scented candle or burning some essential oils to create a sense of calm and serenity. Think of all the things you desire in your career, family, love life, and in all aspects of your life. This will give you a chance to organize your thoughts and have a clear vision of what you want.

Creating the Physical Dream Board

Step 1: Collect all the materials you need.

- Poster board
- A big stack of different magazines (you can get them at libraries, hair salons, dentist offices, the YMCA). Make sure you find lots of different types and subjects. If you limit your options, you'll lose interest after a while.
- Tape
- Glue

Step 2: Go through your magazines and tear images from them. Just have lots of fun looking through magazines and pulling out pictures or words or headlines that catch your eye in a positive way. Have fun with it. Make a big pile of images and phrases and words.

Step 3: Go through the images and lay your favorites on the board. Eliminate any images that no longer feel right. This step is where your intuition comes in. As you lay the pictures on the board, you'll get a sense of how the board should be laid out. For instance, you might assign a theme to each corner of the board—Health, Job, Spirituality, Relationships. It may just be that the images want to go all over the place. Do what feels right.

Step 4: Tape or glue everything onto the board. Add notes if you want. You can paint on it, or write words with markers.

Step 5: Hang your vision board in a place you will see it often.

Virtual Dream Board

I created a virtual dream board on my laptop. This way it's more fluid. I can copy and paste new inspirational photos of things I want to manifest into my life. I peruse the internet for images of my desire and add them under the subjects to which they pertain. Remember this board represents YOU and YOUR desires!

I've categorized my desires in this format:

Title: Career

Insert inspirational photos. Who will you be, how will you feel, and what will you have when your career dreams are your reality?

Title: Desire

I write all the things I want to have happen in my career for the year. Use a bulleted list to organize your ideas.

Title: Why I know I will have this

I write the reasons I know I will have the desires stated above. I add a list of my mentors, organizations I support, and record when I take action based on my mentor's guidance, and when I make contributions.

MY CURRENT VIRTUAL DREAM BOARD FOR SPIRITUALITY

Header: Spirituality

What can I do today to make someone else's life better?

Title: Desires

- I embrace the energy and guidance from my Universal Spirit Guide!
- I am donating massively to my favorite foundations.
- Smile Train: June 23rd, Yancel. Oct 13th, one more!
- Save the Children: Sair in El Salvador monthly contribution
- PAWS monthly contributor
- Joined Organ Donation Foundation Jan 2013
- A Safe Haven Advisory Board Member
- Michael Beckwith Agape Live Streaming Sundays
- Deepak Chopra
- John Of God (Casa de Dom Inacio, Brazil)
- Wayne Dyer: Sep 24th
- Esther Hicks Abraham: March 18th

These are the reasons I want this:

I KNOW these sources guide me into the further enlightenment of my soul.

These are the reasons why I believe I will have this:

I am ready. I am open. I am conscious of being in the Vortex! Because there are no accidents, I am guided on this path and know it is the truest, most authentic fit for me. My path fills my heart and connects me to source energy. All love, all the time!

Look at what Bruce Lee wrote down and then achieved:

> I, Bruce Lee, will be the first highest paid Oriental super star in the United States. In return, I will give the most exciting performances and render the best of quality in the capacity of an actor. Starting 1970 I will achieve world fame and from then onward till the end of 1980 I will have in my possession $10,000,000. I will live the way I please and achieve inner harmony and happiness.

EXERCISE

Now it's time for you to create your dream board. Schedule a date where you can set aside two hours for just you, and commit to creating your physical or virtual vision board.

Joy does not simply happen to us. We have to choose joy and keep choosing it every day.

—Henri Nouwen

• *Chapter Seven* •

COMMUNICATION & RAPPORT

#7 Communication & Rapport

Zig Ziglar, one of the world's great motivational speakers, once said, "People don't care how much you know until they know how much you care." In your quest to embrace your reinvention, I cannot emphasize enough the value of establishing great communication and rapport skills.

We've all had experiences with people where we felt an almost instant feeling of comfort or kindredness. Have you ever thought about why that is? Sometimes, it can be based on pure energy. For example, you observed someone entering a room and they caught your eye, and you had the sense you already knew them, and you had to meet them. It could have been how they carried themselves. It could have been their posture, their smile or their sincere eye contact with someone else in the group. In that particular moment, you may not have been able to pinpoint what it was, you just had a feeling that you liked that person. You may have felt an attraction to them in a romantic way or in a friendly, familial way. You knew you felt something and weren't a hundred percent sure why you felt that way.

People emit and receive energy from one another. The energy you're both emitting, without engaging in a conversation, will cause you to feel good, bad, or indifferent about one another. We also tend to make snap judgments about people based on appearances. For example, if you notice people in a room who have a sloppy appearance, are grossly overweight, have a turned down mouth, sagging posture, weak voice, inability to look you in the eye, or offer a wilted handshake, what are you thinking about them? We intuitively judge people through their energy first and then their appearance.

I'm not saying this is full proof because we've all been guilty of judging a book by its cover and making unfair assessments about people. Still, when someone walks into a room and immediately grabs my attention in a positive way, I usually find I've made a fair assessment of the kind of person they really are.

Apply these tips when establishing rapport in a social setting:

Communicating in Social Settings

1. Prior to the engagement, come up with three or four casual questions to get others talking.
2. Be the first to say "hello." Smile first and shake hands when you meet people.
3. Make an effort to remember people's names and use them frequently.
4. Be an active listener. Give feedback. Maintain eye contact.
5. Listen more than you talk.
6. Stay away from negative and controversial topics and refrain from long-winded stories.
7. Accept people's business cards as if you were given a gift. Read it, and carefully put it away.
8. Act confident and comfortable-even when you're not (act *as if!*).
9. Pay attention to your body language.
10. Do not jump right into other's conversations. Listen, observe, and wait for an opening.

When meeting new people make it your goal to discover:

- Where do they come from?
- Where do they want to go?
- What is their need now?
- How can you help them?

Imagine people you encounter have an invisible sign around their neck that says, "Make me feel important."

I've learned that people will forget what you said,
people will forget what you did, but people will never
forget how you made them feel.

—Maya Angelou

Napoleon Hill, author of the acclaimed book *Think and Grow Rich,* discusses how having a pleasing personality is a characteristic of successful people. What exactly is a pleasing personality? According to Hill, these characteristics are essential to business and personal success in your life and relationships:

- Positive mental attitude
- Flexibility
- Control and direction of enthusiasm
- Sincerity of purpose

People who make you feel good have the characteristics of a pleasing personality. Look again at the qualities listed above. Would you agree that those qualities constitute a pleasing personality?

In my quest to reinvent, create, and expose more of who I am, I like to emulate the same characteristics Hill brought to our attention, and I choose to be around people who embrace those characteristics too.

Find and study successful people you admire, who have the qualities of a pleasing personality that you respond to. Here are some examples from my own list:

Richard Branson

Richard Branson has been described as an extrovert, a man driven by fun and action, people-oriented, and influential. He's an inspiring, charismatic leader as well as entertainer. He's a fearless daredevil and risk-taker. And he's charming, playful, confident, optimistic and caring. He surrounds himself with the right people and then empowers them to create and innovate. The word around the water cooler is that he treats his employees like family.

Nelson Mandela

Nelson Mandela is a great example of a man driven by inspiration to fight injustice and fight for what he believes in. He studied law after witnessing the democracy of African tribal governance at an early age and became a sought after lawyer in Johannesburg, defending black South Africans against government oppression. Because of this opposition and participation in protests, boycotts and insidious organization of native Africans, he was labeled an enemy of the state, accused of treason, disbarred, banned from all political involvement, and sentenced to life in prison. It was his incarceration that brought international attention to the racial injustices of South Africa's Apartheid government. After serving twenty-seven years in prison, he was finally released in 1990, at the age of seventy-two and was elected the first black President of South Africa in 1994. He remains one of the world's most admired political leaders for his strength and perseverance in pursuing justice and freedom, and has been honored with numerous awards including the Nobel Peace Prize.

Maya Angelou

Dr. Maya Angelou is one of the most influential voices of our time. She is a celebrated novelist, poet, educator, producer, actress, historian, filmmaker, and civil rights activist. She grew up in a small community in Stamps, AK where she experienced firsthand the brutality of racial discrimination. In her teenage years, her love for the arts earned her a scholarship to study drama and dance at the San Francisco Labor School. The list of her published verse, non-fiction, and fiction now includes more than thirty bestselling titles. She served on two Presidential committees, was awarded the Presidential Medal of Arts in 2000, the Lincoln Medal in 2008, and has received three Grammy Awards. President Clinton requested that she compose a poem to read at his inauguration in 1993, and Dr. Angelou's reading of her poem *On the Pulse of the Morning* was broadcast live around the world. Her words and actions are a constant source of positive energy.

Dolly Parton

Dolly Parton began her career as a child performer and made her mark in the music world as a country singer and performer. She is a shining example of reinvention, altering course as a country singer, pop star, theme park founder and, back to her bluegrass roots, recording star later in her career. Overall, she has recorded over 3,000 songs and counting. Only time will tell what comes next in her evolving career. The characteristic I admire most in Dolly is her authentic caring spirit. She always maintains a cheerful demeanor and enjoys making people around her feel good.

Communication Styles

After receiving my B.A in Psychology and Master's in Social Science, I was inspired to continue my studies in Neuro-linguistic Programming, Hypnosis and Time-line therapy. While on that course, I was exposed to several methods of assessing personality and communication styles. In my quest to give you great tools that will help you better understand you and the people in your environment I've included a brief summary and web addresses for you to use for your own analysis.

The VAK (Visual-Auditory-Kinesthetic)

The VAK learning styles model and related VAK learning styles tests offer a relatively simple methodology. Therefore, it is important to remember that these concepts and tools are aids to understanding overall personality, preferences and strengths - which is always a mixture in each individual person.

As with any methodology or tool, use VAK and other learning styles ideas with care and interpretation according to the needs of the situation. They are a guide as to the mixture of preferences, strengths and learning styles in an individual, not a basis for deciding on one exclusive preference or approach to the exclusion of everything else.

The VAK learning styles model provides a very easy and quick reference inventory by which to assess people's preferred learning styles, and then most importantly, to design learning methods and experiences that match people's preferences:

- Visual learning style involves the use of seen or observed things, including pictures, diagrams, demonstrations, displays, handouts, films, flip-chart, etc.
- Auditory learning style involves the transfer of information through listening: to the spoken word, of self or others, of sounds and noises.

- Kinesthetic learning involves physical experience - touching, feeling, holding, doing, and practical hands-on experiences.

The word kinesthetic describes the sense of using muscular movement or physical sense. Kinesthesia and kinesthesis are root words, derived from the Greek kineo, meaning move, and aisthesis, meaning sensation. Kinesthetic, therefore, describes a learning style which involves the stimulation of nerves in the body's muscles, joints and tendons. This relates to the colloquial expression "touchy-feely" (kineo-aisthesis = move-sensation).

My Learning Style Results:

Mostly Visual
58% Visual, 25% Auditory and 17% Kinesthetic!

Here is the web address to do your own: http://www.helloquizzy.com/tests/vaktest

Disc Model

About twelve years ago, I completed an online communication survey called the Disc Model and was excited to learn not only about myself but about the communication styles of the people in my life. When you're armed with a better understanding as to how you operate YOU and how to motivate employees, clients and your children, it makes life that much easier.

In the DISC model, there are four basic communication styles. While all of us communicate across each of the four dimensions, we do so to varying degrees. Most of us tend to naturally communicate in one of the four styles most of the time.

Below is a very abbreviated summary of each of the styles. The summary describes the styles when people are at their best and worst in a meeting setting, and offers strategies to prevent trouble in the varying styles.

Hi-D Style

At Their Best

- Driving for efficiency, participating, directing, making direct comments, giving end point first

At Their Worst
- Alienating by being forceful, not letting people catch up, making snap decisions, killing creativity, unaware of what's happening in the group

Strategies
- Keep session fast paced, well planned
- Lay out the process and the benefits
- Get them on your side to go with the flow

Hi-I Style
At Their Best
- Participating, creative, talking, keeping energy up, cheer leading and supporting

At Their Worst
- Don't stop talking, don't listen, don't want to take time for important details, blue-skying, unrealistic

Strategies
- Give lots of chances to talk
- Enlist help for out of the box thinking and getting others to speak
- Have ground rules, keep discussions relevant, end point first, avoid bar discussion

Hi-S Style
At Their Best
- Friendly, supportive, nodding, agreeing, paying attention, good listeners, tolerant, peace makers

At Their Worst
- Going along with what they don't believe, being the silent martyr, checking out, passive- aggressive actions in response to change

Strategies
- Check for agreement
- Use teams to avoid putting on the spot
- Reinforce with praise

Hi-C Style

At Their Best

- Looking at the details, constructive critiquing, identifying impacts of decision, keeping on task, providing a reality check

At Their Worst

- Bogging down in details, giving all the reasons why something won't work, not allowing intuitive judgment, unrealistic expectations of quality

Strategies

- Set the expectation that more detailed analysis will be done outside of the session
- Remind of the level of detail needed for each decision
- Encourage praise first and seeking new solutions

My Personal Disc Result: Hi-I Style

You are socially oriented. You have a strong self-motivation to get to know people in all walks of life and to nurture those relationships. You have a natural enthusiasm for all types of ideas and projects, your own and other people's. People are likely to describe you as gregarious, persuasive and optimistic.

D: Dominance 27%
I: Influencer 58%
S: Steadiness 21%
C: Compliance 5%

Your Assignment:

I recommend doing a survey on yourself and encouraging the people in your environment to do the same. Here is the link: http://discpersonalitytesting.com

The mediocre teacher tells. The good teacher explains. The superior teacher demonstrates. The great teacher inspires.

—William Arthur Ward

Chapter Eight

PEERS & MENTORS

#8 Great Peers & Mentors =
Your Formula for Success

The five people you surround yourself with will be directly proportionate to the level of success you have in all areas of your life. Are you ready to admit that you are completely responsible for the people in your life?

The people around us feed our strength or weaknesses. Answer these questions to help you determine who is in your support circle:

Who are the people that stand in your corner during the most difficult moments?

Which people have risked telling you the hard truth with grace and love simply because they care about you?

Which of your friends refuses to tear down others even when those people are not around?

Who holds you accountable for what you say you are going to do?

With whom do you feel safe?

Poor peer groups:
- More critical than encouraging or complimentary
- Belittle and laugh at your dreams and goals
- Embarrass and humiliate you
- Siphon your time and energy

Great peer groups:
- Speak words that build your confidence
- See the validity and beauty of your dreams and goals
- They get excited about your potential

- They remind you of your special gifts and talents
- They see your strengths
- They respect what you have done and where you came from
- They are good listeners and are sincerely interested in you
- They live by their rules and don't expect you to follow them
- They are at peace with themselves, so they don't have to prove anything to you
- They are authentic and don't lie to you to feed your ego

Client Story

Jason had the dilemma of keeping or dissolving his relationship with his cousin, Bill. It was tricky because Jason and Bill had been business partners until Jason bought out Bill's share of the company because of his unscrupulous business practices.

Jason maintained his social life with Bill and had recovered from his disappointment about the business aspect of their relationship, but was still dealing with Bill's constant jabs about cutting him out. When I asked Jason if he had seen signs prior to getting into business with Bill regarding his unscrupulous behavior, Jason said yes. He attempted to justify why he thought Bill would be a great business partner. When he finished, I asked him if Bill was trustworthy. Jason swallowed hard before replying that he wasn't. I then asked, "Would you allow your son to hang out with a person who had Bill's characteristics?" He again answered no.

I shared my favorite Wayne Dyer quote with him: "Love your family. Choose your friends." You can love your family, and be there for them in emergencies, but you have complete autonomy in choosing who belongs in your sacred peer space. Jason made the decision to spend less time with Bill socially, allowing him to create new friendships and nurture some of his other social friendships at a higher level.

My Story

I was in the third grade when I remember my Mother saying "I don't want you playing with Jenny."

I knew Jenny was trouble. She was tough and "boy-crazy" like my mother said, but I was pulled toward the excitement surrounding Jenny's daring behavior.

I continued to play with Jenny without my mother knowing for several months. One day, during some child-hood playground drama, Jenny turned on me and beat me up. I was so hurt and humiliated. I didn't tell my mother, but I guess I needed to experience my own lumps to get the lesson. Mom was right, and I ended the friendship with Jenny.

By fifth grade, I developed a relationship with a girl down the street who became my best friend. I admired her intelligence, her passion and self-discipline toward dance and piano lessons. Her influence in my life was a major catalyst toward my desire to excel academically and intellectually.

Can you think of peers from your youth that influenced you in a negative way and ones who influenced you positively?

As you mature, you realize the importance of sharing your valuable time with people who are going to respect you, positively influence you, and be there for you no matter what. It's up to you to choose the groups you spend your precious time with. If you give time to those unworthy of it, stop complaining. You are the one who gave them your time. They abused it because you allowed them the opportunity. Become more selective. Remember, the same time you waste on a poor peer group could have been invested with winners.

Think about who your peers are today, and ask yourself the following questions:

- Are they your life-long friends from grade school or high school?
- Are they your college friends?
- Are they work colleagues?
- Think about why you chose them as friends in the first place.
- Are they the same person they were when you first met them?
- Have they matured?
- Do you still get value from their presence in your life?
- Are they a pain in the butt?
- Do you hang onto the relationship out of duty?

On your quest to reinvent yourself, it's important that your peers respect and honor your new journey. Look at the list below for tips that will help you show up in a way that will attract a quality peer group.

1. Relationships give you permission to tell your story and help your dreams come alive. The more people you meet, the more you can change the world, both through helping others and spreading your ideas.

2. Ask someone to tell their story. Everyone is dying to get their message out to the world; they just might not know it. Give them permission, get present and simply listen.

3. Be genuine and vulnerable. When meeting someone, lead with intimacy. Humanize it! Don't rattle off how great you are, and all the things you've done. Bragging will only distance you. Be humble. Tell them the scary story of what shaped your life and what got you here. We all have defining personal moments in our life.

4. Walk into a room and see friends not strangers. I don't care if you don't recognize a single face in the room. Adopt the belief that these people all want to connect as much as you do. Because it's true. Walk up and see how you can help. See friends, and friends they will become.

5. Be a host at your own party. Invite groups who don't know one another so you can create new connections. When you're a host, do everything you can to make others feel welcome. Do this with those close to you and those you want to be close to. Make it fun. Sit strangers together.

6. Be a host at everyone else's party. Being a host at your own home is a given. What about other parties you go to? The job of a host is to make others feel welcome and accommodated. Why only do this in your own home? Look at every interaction as a chance to be a host. Ask, "How can I help you?" Have fun with it.

7. Get rid of people who don't contribute to your dreams. Your peer group is your choice. Choose wisely. We all have people who put us down or don't believe in our ideas. They suck energy and diminish our potential. Who says you have to be around them? You don't, so stop acting like you do.

8. Repair bad connections. For whatever reason there are people in our lives we cannot get away from, who seem to be out to get us. Kill them with kindness. Be the bigger person and do the following. First, feel their pain—try to empathize and somehow see their side.

Second, be complementary–tell them what you respect about them. You can always find something. Relate to them. Often, they'll become extremely close to you because you're the first person to help them through their insecurity.

9. Choose to care about someone. The easiest way to get you to care about me is for me to care about you. Do what you can to help those around you.

10. Spend routine quality time. Notice the people you come across. It may be the shop owner down the street, your mother, long lost friend or your favorite author. Write them into your story. Set up group dinners, cook for them, plan a trip to the amusement park or rent out a paintball field.

11. Get lost in conversation for hours. Make these interactions a weekly routine. There's nothing more important. When you find someone new and interesting, invite them to events right away to make them feel a part of your life. They won't forget it.

12. Find groups in town. Make this a priority. There are like-minded people all over your town. Search out those groups. Check Craig's List, MeetUp, coffee shop bulletin boards, Chambers of Commerce, Twitter, Facebook Groups, LinkedIn groups.

Take a look at the mindset strategies of successful and unsuccessful people to see how you are showing up in life.

SUCCESSFUL PEOPLE	UNSUCCESSFUL PEOPLE
Schedule their time	Freeform and wander throughout the day
Forgive others	Hold a grudge
Have a sense of gratitude	Have a sense of entitlement
Talk about ideas	Talk about people
Share information and data	Horde information and data
Exude joy	Exude anger

Set goals and make plans	Never set goals or do any planning
Embrace change	Fear change
Give others credit for their victories	Take all the credit for their victories
Accept responsibility	Blame others
Read every day	Almost never read
Keep a journal	Tell others they journal but really do not
Keep a to-do list	Fly by the seat of their pants
Continuously learn	Think they know it all
Want others to succeed	Want others to fail
Compliment	Criticize
Exude joy and positivity	Exude anger and negativity

You are the average of the five people closest to you.
—Jim Rohn

Life is no fun alone. Experiences, accomplishments and success don't mean much of anything if you're alone at home with no one to celebrate with. What makes going to a restaurant, bar or a new place so much fun? For the most part, it's the people—either the ones you know or the ones you meet. Be intentional about nurturing these relationships. Stay genuine. If you don't currently have a network full of passionate inspiring people, then create it. Start with the people you spend most your time with, then move outwards.

Without this support, you'll likely never do the groundbreaking things you're here to do. It's the biggest reason people don't leap. People around them think they're crazy and, before you know it, you think you're crazy too. All of a sudden, you're back to doing what everyone else is doing.

Create a network people dream of. Welcome the challenge. You can have it. You just have to cultivate it. Surround yourself with people who light you on fire. You will fuel one another and the world will be better.

Mentors

> *Treat people as if they were what they ought to be*
> *and you help them to become what they are capable*
> *of being.*
>
> **—Goethe**

The original Mentor is a character in Homer's epic poem *The Odyssey*. When Odysseus, King of Ithaca went to fight in the Trojan War, he entrusted the care of his kingdom to Mentor. Mentor served as the teacher and overseer of Odysseus's' son, Telemachus.

Merriam-Webster defines a mentor as "a trusted counselor or guide." A mentor is an individual, usually older, always more experienced, who helps and guides another individual's development. This guidance is not done for personal gain. They are people who see more talent and ability within you, than you see in yourself, and help bring it out of you. They are wise, loyal advisors or coaches.

There are two types of mentors. Mentors in your immediate surroundings and virtual mentors—people, living or dead, that you admire and would like to emulate.

Mentors Qualities to Look For

Experienced–Mentors are typically older, but that is not a rule.

Similar Goals–Find a mentor that has goals similar to yours. It can only help your chances of success if your mentor has already gone through a lot of the work you have in front of you.

Availability–Your mentor needs to be available for interaction. It can be great to have a really successful person mentoring you, but if they aren't available to meet, it defeats the purpose of the arrangement.

Caring–We all want people to think what we're doing is important, especially our mentor. A mentor needs to care about your success just as much as you do. This is a person that should help you up when you fall. All of this starts with the mentor caring about you and your success.

Positive–Your mentor needs to be positive and help keep you positive. If you spend a meaningful amount of time with your mentor, and they are positive, this is bound to rub off on you. Remember, good thoughts in, good thoughts out. People want to work with other positive people.

Focus–You want a mentor who is able to focus on you and what you would like to achieve, and who will help you focus.

Trustworthy–A mentor-protégé relationship is most beneficial when you can share experiences and bits of information that a normal acquaintance wouldn't know about you. Openness and honesty also help build credibility and trust between the mentor and protégé.

Why a Mentor

> *Tell me and I forget, teach me and I may remember, involve me and I learn.*
>
> **—Benjamin Franklin**

A mentor can give you the benefit of his or her perspective and experience. He or she can help you assimilate to a new position and give you an insider's view on how to get things done. A mentor can also help you look at situations in new ways. He or she can ask hard questions and help you solve problems. When you struggle to believe in yourself, in your ability to overcome a challenge, the mentor is able to ask those tough questions that trigger a necessary change in thinking.

A mentor can help you define your career path and ensure that you don't lose focus and continue down that road even when you become distracted by day-to-day pressures. You need to own your career plan and learn to balance the day-to-day with the big picture. You always have to look at where you're going and how you are trying to develop yourself.

When you know you are meeting with your mentor, you ensure that all the tasks you discussed in your last meeting are completed. You fall into the habit of holding yourself accountable for completing your action items. Then the excitement of completing tasks and seeing the results motivates you even more to hold yourself accountable and strive for achievements you previously thought were impossible.

A mentor can be a great sounding board for all issues, whether you are having difficulty with your immediate supervisor, an ethical dilemma, or need advice on how to tackle a new project or ask for a raise. Mentors share their stories and experiences and expect to keep it within the boundaries of the relationship. Be sure you maintain confidences.

A mentor who knows you well can be a strong champion of your positive attributes and an ally during any bumpy spots in your career. It is important to build trust and prove yourself worthy. Mentors should encourage you to share your story and share yourself. It's hard to champion someone if you don't know who they are. You bring who you are to what you do.

A mentor can help expand your network of contacts and business acquaintances. A mentor can open doors within your company, in other companies, or onto a board.

A mentor whose work you admire can be a strong inspiration. Your mentor must be a respected member of the community and the business world. You will be associated with the reputation of this person. Don't pick purely on the basis of power.

With the help of a good mentor, you can work more efficiently with a clearer view of the future you are trying to achieve. This helps you feel more confident in your job, which leads to better job performance and more success along your chosen path.

> *People inspire you or they drain you, pick them wisely.*
>
> **—Hans F. Hansen**

EXERCISE

Can you think of people that have had a positive impact on you? In the spaces below, jot down the names of these people and a quick note about what it was about them that made an impression on you.

Who are five people you admire and why?

1. _____
   _____
   _____

2. _____
   _____
   _____

3. _____
   _____
   _____

4. _____
   _____
   _____

5. _____
   _____
   _____

In Chapter 1, I discussed several high achievers who have figured out ways to reinvent themselves repeatedly with a record of accomplishment for success. Once people have achieved this high level of success, they tend to be drawn toward a path of self-actualization.

Wouldn't it be wise to start assimilating these characteristics even before you've achieved your greatest success as a means to enhance the journey?

> *Everyone with rare exception knows that you attract into your life a reflection of what you think. But, you also attract into your life what you judge. If you think men are players, you attract players, if you think people are dishonest, you attract dishonest people. If you are focused on a sickness or disease, you attract more. If you focus on poverty or lack, you gain nothing more than an empty bank account. Everything you hold in your conscious thought becomes your cage and your reality. Why not fake it until you make it folks. See abundance, see honesty in all, embrace good healthy, emotionally healthy people, focus on the beauty and not the ugly. And for crying out loud fix what hurts you, heal what aches, mend your mind and restore it to perfection. You were born of perfection, it is your core. Meditate, exercise, eat nutritionally and address what you are harboring, then you will attract lovely all day long.*
>
> **—Ariaa Jaeger**

Everyone needs a coach, whether it's a top level executive, a graduate student, a homemaker, a homeless person or the President of the United States.

—Anthony Robbins

• *Chapter Nine* •

REINFORCEMENT COACHING

#9 Reinforcement-Coaching

Would you agree that people are more effective when they are being held accountable? If your parents didn't tell you to clean your room as a child, there's a very good chance your bedroom would have been condemned by a violation from the health department. We all need a good kick in the butt every now and then to get real about our lives and to stay the course.

Client Story

John, a financial services provider, discovered he felt happiest when he was taking urban-style photographs. He spent all of his spare time riding trains and taking buses to gritty neighborhoods snapping pictures.

> **John**: I love photography. I have thousands of images on my laptop from the last two years that I haven't done anything with.
>
> **Me**: Walk me through the experience of a photography session. I'd like you help me understand how you prep for the event, how you choose where to go and how you decide what to shoot.

When I help people get attached or re-attached to doing something they love, it's important for the person to immerse themselves back into the experience. I want them to feel the feelings of being in the moment, re-living the experience through detailed memories. On occasion, I'll have my client answer a series of questions about something specific in writing as a homework assignment. Other times, it is important for me to ask questions in person to note the passion, the silences, the enthusiasm and the trepidation I hear in their voices.

John: I have a large map in my living room and I use green stickpins for the places I plan to visit. I then change them to red once I've visited the place. If I want to visit the place again in a different lighting, setting or season because I really enjoyed it, I use a yellow stickpin. Then I grab my backpack, pack my equipment, and a few snacks, and head out.

Me: Do you have an intention when you arrive at your destination?

John: You're gonna probably laugh when I tell you, but when I arrive I put on my playlist and pretend I'm on an assignment for some edgy urban art magazine. Sometimes I even put extra pressure on myself to get in and out in ninety minutes like it's a war zone and I need to get the best shots as fast as possible.

Me: I love it, John. You sound like you're more than the average artist. You desire a sense of pressure by imposing a fictitious danger to your work.

John: Exactly. I think I get the best shots when I'm pumped listening to my music and have a deadline.

Me: What do people say when they see your photos?

John: I've only showed them to a few friends and they like them. I showed my mother once, but she doesn't get it. (Laughs) She wants me to take pictures of nature and trees.

Me: Do you see yourself selling your work or having it admired in a gallery?

John: That would be great, but I have no idea how I would do that.

Me: Could you see yourself doing photography full-time?

John: Definitely! I have so many ideas about the types of shots I want to do and places I'd like to visit across the U.S.

Me: Do you have any photographers you admire?

John: Yeah of course. He's the reason I started taking pictures. I met him at University three years ago. He showed me his stuff, and I bought my photography equipment soon after that.

Me: Are you still in touch with him?

John: I bumped into him a year-and-a-half ago and told him that I started taking pictures because of him. He was flattered.

Me: Do you believe your work is at his level?

John: I never looked at it like that.

Me: What would it take for you to feel confident enough to sell your work?

John: I'm not sure.

I asked John those last few questions to learn how confident he was with his work. I also wanted to find out if he had a mentor that would be willing to let John shadow him to learn techniques, share business tips, and add to John's self-esteem.

John rekindled his relationship with his mentor who referred him to another photographer who permitted John to shadow him as an apprentice. That inspired him to work with models on photo shoots in urban environments. He soon was being paid to take his pictures, and attracting his own clients, soon signing a full-time contract with a successful photographer. John broadened his niche to include models. He takes many assignments in rural settings and loves his life. Never say never!

> *Each problem has hidden in it an opportunity so powerful that it literally dwarfs the problem. The greatest success stories were created by people who recognized a problem and turned it into an opportunity.*
>
> **—Joseph Sugarman**

My Story

When I was in The U.S. Air Force at nineteen, I had several supervisors. I quickly learned that while I wasn't given choices about whom I reported to, I could "take the best and leave the rest". As I shared in *Undercover Angel*, my first supervisor made it known that she was not my fan. This taught me a new way to cope with people who are not going to be my supporters in life.

There were several choices I could have made—make a formal complaint, re-attempt reconciliation with my supervisor, or make the best of my present condition by focusing on the big picture. I chose the last method. When I focused on finding ways to have a cheerful disposition in spite of the not-so-great work environment, I found I had won. I was empowered with the belief that I had complete control of my attitude.

When I was assigned to my new supervisor, a year later, I realized I now was in the presence of a mentor. Staff Sergeant Ricky Hawes embraced all of the qualities and values I revered in an individual. He was extremely intelligent, was an excellent communicator and had an unparalleled work ethic. SSgt. Hawes' customer service standards were impeccable. Because he was a man's man, someone who got into the trenches with his troops, his underlings couldn't help but want to perform at their best. Our goal was to do our jobs so well that it made him look good. We all wanted to be a reflection of him.

Working for SSgt Hawes, I began to care about things that I once felt were insignificant. For instance, one of my earlier duties was detailing the base commander's vehicle. I soon discovered what detailing really meant when I was given cotton swabs to dust the air vents, Armor All to clean the tracks at the bottom of the vehicle doors, rubbing alcohol to remove specs from the front bumper, and upholstery cleaner to revitalize the seats. To get to a place where I felt trivial things such as these were important was a character and value reinvention.

What Hawes instilled in me was the desire to do great work regardless of how trivial I thought it was. He explained that my name would be attached to the job and asked what my name meant to me. What standard did I have for who I was and how I showed up in life? I'm certain that it was because I adopted his standards and value system that I received the title of Airman of the Year in the U.S. Air Force.

I've seen the power of Life Coaching firsthand and I know how beneficial it can be.
—Leeza Gibbons

In Chapter 7, you mapped out your vision in the various categories of your life. Now, consider which people inspire you in areas you'd like to achieve. You might consider a person who has passed on, a hero, or perhaps someone you admire but haven't met. You can plug in your mentors, the coaches you already have, and the coaches you'd like to have, to assist you in getting the results you're looking for.

In Chapter 3, I referenced how I got leverage on myself through committing to a date to publish my first book after a discussion with my author Mastermind group. The value of a Mastermind group is priceless. These are the people who you respect, admire and value. They could be in your neighborhood or living in another country. With technology today, using Skype, online meetings, and video chat, the gatherings are accessible to everyone with a computer.

> *At times, our own light goes out and is rekindled by a spark from another person. Each of us has cause to think with deep gratitude of those who have lighted the flame within us.*
>
> **—Albert Schweitzer**

You can have a Mastermind group in virtually all areas of your life: They enhance your life experience through your sharing your opinions, experiences, and expertise with people who have similar passions.

EXERCISE

Start creating your Mastermind groups. Write down the names of at least three people in each group. Add more names if they readily come to mind.

Health Mastermind?

_____
_____
_____
_____
_____
_____

Career Mastermind

_____
_____
_____
_____
_____

Emotional Mastermind

_____
_____
_____
_____
_____

Relationship Mastermind

Spiritual Mastermind

Hobby Mastermind (writing, reading clubs, film clubs, wine clubs, philosophy, art, knitting, sculpting, sports, cooking, travel, other)

Now that you have assigned the people to your groups begin to coordinate monthly or quarterly meetings. In those meeting, s you'll want to share your goals, support one another's ideas, and encourage a setting of creativity and most important accountability. The most accountable people to themselves and others hold the keys to the most success. It's that simple!

> *You have to believe it's possible and believe in yourself. Because after you've decided what you want, you have to believe it's possible and possible for you, not just for other people. Then you need to seek out models, mentors, and coaches.*

—Jack Canfield

Coaching with Lisa Lockwood

When I choose to take on a personal client for Reinvention Coaching, I send them an intake questionnaire to best prepare for our first session. Here is a sample of my intake questionnaire and the types of questions I ask of my new clients.

LISA LOCKWOOD CONSULTING REINVENTION COACHING QUESTIONNAIRE

Please take the time necessary to fill out this form. Answer honestly and openly without editing your thoughts. The time and energy invested in this process will increase the quality and results of the coaching experience you will have. Once completed, please return to the following email address: Lisa@LisaLockwood.com

1. Personal Information

Name:

Phone Numbers

Home:

Cell:

Home Address:

Business Address:

Email:

Your Age:

Marital Status (if in a relationship, since when?):

Name of your Partner:

Names & Ages of Children:

2. What is your occupation? Briefly describe what you do.

Occupation:

Description:

3. Is this the occupation of your dreams?

Answer:

4. What are you most proud of accomplishing to this point in your life?

Answer:

What is the most difficult experience you have overcome?

Answer:

5. What is your life vision? In other words for you "the dream that would never end"?

Answer:

6. Your Mission: What type of effect or change would you like to create in the world with your life?

Answer:

7. Passion: (Love of something) what do you have an extreme calling to do. In other words, it is not work, it comes easy for you to do it, and you are happy doing it?

Answer:

8. What does commitment mean to you?

Answer:

9. What does accountability mean to you?

Answer:

10. What results are you looking for from coaching?

Answer:

11. For your regular coaching calls/sessions, would you prefer days or evenings?

Answer:

12. Your Issue: What single issue drains your energy the most? What would most dramatically change your entire quality of life if you could wake up, and it was perfect?

Answer:

Other almost as important issues:

13. Are you committed to doing the work between coaching calls/ sessions (i.e. filling in a worksheet before each call/session, exercises)?

Answer:

14. What else do we need to know to ensure you achieve maximum results? (For example, I have a health, learning or attention issue that makes life a little more challenging for me. I need a coach who is firm but sensitive or someone who is encouraging but really pushes me. I need someone who can help me brainstorm and sort out all my ideas. I need someone who can help create clarity and focus, etc).

Answer:

15. Rate yourself in these specific areas of your life from 0-10, 0 being the lowest and 10 being the highest.

Question: Health

Answer:

Question: Hobbies (Doing things just for fun).

Answer:

Question: Career

Answer:

Question: Financial (How satisfied are you with what your current status)?

Answer:

Question: Intimate Relationship

Answer:

Question: Family & Friends

Answer:

Question: Spirituality (Your connection with self, nature/God)

Answer:

Question: Emotions (Are you living in the emotions you want?)

Answer:

16. Education/Business Background: What type of formal education, professional courses and experience do you have?

Answer:

Thank you for investing the time and energy to fill out this questionnaire. The information provided will be kept confidential and will serve in creating a positive and results-oriented coaching experience. I look forward to the privilege of working with you.

Lisa Lockwood Consulting

After I receive my client's responses, we schedule a date for our first session together. In that session, I'm able to get a feel for the direction the client wants to head. I know what is expected of me, and the client has a baseline of my coaching protocol. My clients are given "fun work" assignments to complete before our next live scheduled session. One of the assignments is to fill in another questionnaire so that I may track their progress as well as where they may have fallen short. Here is an example of the follow-up questionnaire.

Coaching Session Date:

What was the most challenging about the last week? What can I DO to overcome those challenges? (Delegate, accountability, explore the whys, let them go.)
1.
2.
3.

What did I learn about myself this week? What did I notice about my ways of being? (Happy, sad, positive, powerful, friendly, open, negative, joyful, enthusiastic, depressed, shut-down, etc.)
1.
2.
3.

What am I thankful for this week? Did I express my gratitude in some way?
1.
2.
3.

What opportunities are available to me now? What do I intend to DO about these opportunities?
1.
2.
3.

What are the biggest challenges I face in the next week? What do I intend to DO about these challenges?
1.
2.
3.

What results do I want from this coaching session? What kind of support am I seeking? 1. 2. 3.
My action commitments or homework before the next session: 1. 2. 3.
Next Session Date: Time:

After coaching thousands of people, I have found there are seven stumbling blocks that prevent people from getting the results they truly want in life. I have made those stumbling blocks and the solutions available to you. Please go to www.LisaLockwood.com and receive my FREE report.

Acknowledging the good that you already have in your life is the foundation for all abundance.

—Eckhart Tolle

• *Chapter Ten* •

BE GRATEFUL

 # 10 Gratitude

Gratitude. What does gratitude mean to you? According to Cicero, "Gratitude is not only the greatest of the virtues, but the parent of all others".

When undergoing any intentional shift, change or reinvention, the first step is awareness. It's essential to recognize a pattern in your former way of thinking. As soon as the old pattern arises, stop in the moment, see it for what it is, and immediately apply the new pattern you'd like to implement.

One way to accomplish this is to talk about your blessings more than you talk about your problems. What we focus upon manifests itself in our lives. Gratitude keeps us physically healthy, spiritually strong, emotionally open, and available to all life's opportunities.

> *For each new morning with its light, for rest and shelter of the night, for health and food, for love and friends, for everything Thy goodness sends.*
> **—Ralph Waldo Emerson**

My day begins always begins with puppy love and I never grow weary of it. From the moment of my first stretch, I'm met by my puppy who crawls her way up to my head and plants kisses on my face. At the sound of my first words, usually, "Good morning Pinky-boo," her tail wags with vigor and she nuzzles into my neck for a few moments before flopping onto her back for her anticipated tummy rub. How can my day not be great with a wake-up like that?

What is your morning ritual? A blaring alarm or do you have an internal clock? Are you greeted with the sun peeping through your window or a warm embrace from your significant other? Figure out a way to have your welcome into the new day be significant and special to set the tone for what is to come.

As I progress through my morning, I'm visually stimulated by the things I've used to decorate my personal environment. Directly across from my bed hangs the word "Love" in hot pink. I look at that word and instantly feel warm inside. As I brush my teeth, I look at my Hello Kitty bubble bath bottle and feel joy. I read The Prayer of Jabez, "Oh that you would bless me indeed and expand my territory, that your hand would be with me to keep me from evil that I may not cause pain" that has been mounted on my bathroom mirror for the last ten years.

As I prepare my morning greens, I listen to *You Take My Breath Away* by Sarah Brightman and then I scroll through my Virtual Vision Board so that my desires are always top of my mind. I then intermittently dance and play with my puppy before prepping for my day.

Before bed, I again play some beautiful music—my favorite is the *Conversations with God* CD—and then I add some of the "highs" of my day that I feel grateful for to my Vision Board. I set an intention for the next day and read some of my favorite incantations that I've included here for you.

My Incantations
All that I need to know
at any given moment is revealed to me.
I trust myself and trust life.
All is well.

I breathe in the fullness & richness of life.
I observe with joy as life abundantly supports me
and supplies me with more good than I can imagine.
Everything is working out for my highest good.
Out of this situation, only good will come.

I do not have to earn love.
I am loveable because I exist.
Others reflect the love that I have for myself.

My income is constantly increasing.
I begin now, today, to open myself to ever increasing prosperity.

An attitude of gratitude draws the mind closer to the source from which all blessings come.
—Wallace Wattles

Expressing gratitude is a lot more than saying thank you. People who are grateful have been found to be happier, more energetic, hopeful, and report experiencing more frequent positive emotions. They tend to be more helpful and empathetic, more spiritual and religious, more forgiving, and less materialistic. The more a person is inclined to express gratitude, the less likely they are to be depressed, anxious, lonely or envious.

Think about things that have happened in your life that were not so great. In hindsight, can you, or have you already, attached a new empowering meaning to them? To help guide you in this process, consider looking at the disempowering scenario from a place of gratitude.

After everything you have learned thus far, will you consider attaching better meanings to not-so-great events and life experiences more rapidly? Why wait weeks, months, or even years to set yourself free of the grief surrounding a not-so-great event?

Helen Keller remarked, "I have always thought it would be a blessing if each person could be blind and deaf for a few days during his early adult life. Darkness would make him appreciate sight; silence would teach him the joys of sound".

I understand Helen Keller's desire to make people more aware of what they already have by temporarily taking away what they take for granted, albeit extreme and not the most feasible option. I do recommend just taking a few moments each day to think about what it would be like to lose a sense, a freedom or an ability that you may take for granted. There is ALWAYS something to be thankful for!

Client Story

I often receive beautiful testimonials from coaching clients. It is refreshing and humbling to receive word on a past client's progress. Recently, a client from Quebec reached out to me on Facebook to tell me that I had given her the personal strength and courage to open her own coffee house. Despite being educated in one field, but wanting to do something completely different, she went with her instinct and invested in a holistic coffee shop. Four years later, the coffee shop is flourishing, she's extremely happy, and recently entered a contest for local businesses in her region.

Receiving news like that, out-of-the-blue, is such a beautiful gift. It also reminds me of the impact I can have and fuels me to continue to do what I do best—bring people back to joy by re-attaching them to doing what they love as a career. Moments like these make me grateful beyond words.

This year, I decided to do an online gratitude journal that I referenced above in addition to the vision map I shared with you in Chapter 7. It's as simple as writing the date and listing one event or experience that happened that day that you are grateful for. I love to scroll back and look at the items I've listed to flood myself with the same emotion I experienced the day I wrote it. There are so many ways for you to experience gratitude. This is just one quick way to refocus your mindset.

My Online Gratitude Journal Entries:

- January 7: Tackled every item on my to-do list and still had time to have a puppy play date!
- Feb 26: A coaching client just incorporated her business and is over the moon with joy.
- June 3: Received $5500.00 refund from the IRS for an overpayment!
- Aug19: Was booked for a National TV Interview!

Project What You Expect

I also like to project what I'd like to have happen. So, occasionally, I will postdate my gratitude list with a random date in the future and mark down the dollar sign symbol to indicate I'd like to receive unexpected money that day:

- March 3: $$$$$$$$

Or, I'll write a date and whatever I'd like to have happen:

- July 2: Surprising good news!

Getting Yourself Back Into a Good Emotional State

I encourage you try this experiment. Think about an event that causes you a feeling of minor distress. Sit with that emotion for a moment, then immediately shift your focus to another event in your life that causes you joy and happiness. Think of anything you are grateful for in your life. Notice how fast you can shift your mood by focusing on things you are grateful for.

Remember, if you are criticizing, you are not being grateful. If you are blaming, you are not being grateful. If you are complaining, you are not being grateful. If you are feeling tension, you are not being grateful. If you are rushing, you are not being grateful. If you are in a bad mood, you are not being grateful.

Gratitude can transform your life. Are you allowing minor things to get in the way of your transformation and the life you deserve?

One of my favorite mentors, Anthony Robbins, who I've had the pleasure of working with and for since 2001 does a gratitude exercise that he recently shared on Oprah Winfrey's Life Class series called an Emotional Flood. The purpose is to get people back into their heart space in order to appreciate themselves and their experiences fully. I've provided an excerpt for you to read. I further recommend you finding it on YouTube so you can close your eyes and completely focus on the experience.

Emotional Flood by Anthony Robbins

Put your hands on your heart. Close your eyes. And all we're going to do is we're going to journey into all the things you feel grateful about, but first, physically feel your heart.

Breathe deep in your heart. Feel the power of your heart. Feel the strength of your heart, feel grateful for your heart and what it's guided you to do in this life, to give and to be. You didn't have to buy this heart. You didn't have to earn it. Somebody thought enough of you to give you this gift of life without doing anything instantly when you were born. As long as it beats you are alive. Right now step into a moment in your life that you can feel deep feelings of gratitude for, any moment at all from your childhood or as an adult.

Breathe in your heart, step in that moment and see what you saw then hear what you heard then and feel what you felt then, right now.

Feel so grateful; feel that moment was sacred, that it was blessed and that you were blessed. Take it in, don't just think it, see it, feel it, be there.

Now reach out and bring in another memory that you can be grateful for, any moment at all, just bring it into your heart on top of the one that's already there. Step in and feel the power and grace of that moment.

And bring a third moment in, maybe this moment can be a coincidence. We all love coincidence because we did nothing for it. Something just happened. You met somebody you went somewhere, and it lead to something magnificent in your life, something you are so grateful for—a person a relationship, an insight, a life change. Step into the gratitude of that moment and feel it as well.

Take your hand off your heart and just continue to breathe and go on a journey of moments of your life you're grateful for feeling each one in your body like you are there.

And now shift to a moment you are proud about. Quickly we are going to do moments rapidly just reach out and grab a moment in your life you are proud about. Bring in a moment you're proud about. Someone you're proud of, your children, yourself, bring that into your heart a moment of pride, feeling proud. Breathe the way you do when you feel proud. Along with gratitude, think of something you accomplished in your life small or big that you feel proud about, and bring that in.

Think of a romantic or sensual or sexy moment and bring that in too on top of the things you are grateful for on top of things you're proud about, a sexy moment a sensual moment, and a romantic moment. Bring in a moment that made you laugh out loud. Did you ever laugh so hard that milk came out your nose or something like that? Bring it in your heart when you felt this incredible laughter over something so silly.

Bring in a special moment with family and a friend. A moment that's magical to you. Bring that into your heart as well and stack it on top of the all the others.

Bring in a moment now that was pure excitement. Make the sound that you do when you do when you're excited. Bring that in your body. Make that sound of excitement out loud.

And now for 10 seconds just reach out and bring in moments from the future like getting an advance view of what's coming, moments of love, moments of excitement , moments of romance, moments of accomplishment, bring 'em in fast. Bring your hands in ten times real quick. Bring them in and at the end just shout the word Yes! Say yes! How many of you thought about things you haven't thought about in a long time?

Now when you accompany this process with music, your eyes closed and the sound of a powerful voice guiding you through, you will receive the optimal benefit of this exercise as I have many times over.

I think the most fitting way to express an aspect of my spirituality is to share a value I hold true in my identity.

Give Joy!

Every single day, no matter who you meet in the day—friends, family, work colleagues, strangers—give joy to them. Give a smile or a compliment or kind words or kind actions, but give joy! Do your best to make sure that every single person you meet has a better day because they saw you. This might sound like it is not connected with you and your life, but believe me it is inseparably connected through cosmic law.

> *As you give joy to every person you meet, you bring joy to YOU. The more you can give joy to others, the more you will bring the joy back to you.*
> **—Rhonda Byrnes,** *The Secret*

Thank you for dedicating your time reading *Reinventing YOU*. My hope is that you have been given more clarity as to your life's mission and are anxious to Reinvent YOU into the person you were meant to be.

Be well, friend!

An attitude of gratitude draws the mind closer to the source from which all blessings come.

—Wallace Wattles

Cultivate the habit of being grateful for every good thing that comes to you, and to give thanks continuously. And because all things have contributed to your advancement, you should include all things in your gratitude.

—Ralph Waldo Emerson

Do not spoil what you have by desiring what you have not; remember that what you now have was once among the things you only hoped for.

—Epicurus

We can only be said to be alive in those moments when our hearts are conscious of our treasures.

—Thornton Wilder

Gratitude in advance is the most powerful creative force in the universe.

—Neale Donald Walsch

Are any of these 7 stumbling blocks
holding you back from grabbing YOUR brass ring?

After coaching thousands of people, I have found there are seven stumbling
blocks that prevent people from getting the results they truly want in life.

FIRST THING..HONOR THE STUMBLING BLOCKS
They are letting you know you are close to victory!

SECOND THING... DOWNLOAD YOUR BONUS MATERIAL
that identifies the blocks...

AND...MORE IMPORTANTLY...
tells you exactly what to do to
REMOVE and EXTINGUISH the blocks
so you can move forward and celebrate your life!

Go to

www.lisalockwood.com

and receive my Bonus Report

valued at $497

for FREE now!

A portion of all of Lisa

Lockwood's proceeds go to her

favorite Charities

Smile Train, Paws & A Safe Haven

pets are worth saving

Printed in the USA
CPSIA information can be obtained
at www.ICGtesting.com
JSHW082207140824
68134JS00014B/477

9 781614 485506